Why Me?

Understanding One's Worldly Fate

OMAR SULEIMAN

KUBE PUBLISHING

In association with

YAQEEN™
INSTITUTE FOR ISLAMIC RESEARCH

Why Me?
Understanding One's Worldly Fate

First published in England by
Kube Publishing Ltd
Markfield Conference Centre
Ratby Lane, Markfield
Leicestershire, LE67 9SY
United Kingdom

Tel: +44 (0) 1530 249230
Website: www.kubepublishing.com
Email: info@kubepublishing.com

Cataloguing-in-Publication Data is available from the British Library.

ISBN 978-1-84774-255-1 Casebound
eISBN 978-1-84774-256-8 Ebook

Proofreading and editing: Wordsmiths
Cover design, typesetting and calligraphy: Jannah Haque
Printed by: IMAK Ofset, Turkey.

Transliteration Guide

A brief guide to some of the letters and symbols used in the Arabic transliteration in this book.

th	ث	*ḥ*	ح	*dh*	ذ
ṣ	ص	*ḍ*	ض	*ṭ*	ط
ẓ	ظ	ʿ	ع	ʾ	ء

ā	ـَا آ	*ī*	ـِي	*ū*	ـُو

ﷺ May the peace and blessings of Allah be upon him.	عَزَّ وَجَلَّ Glorified and Majestic (is He).	رَضِيَ ٱللَّٰهُ عَنْهُ May Allah be pleased with him.
رَضِيَ ٱللَّٰهُ عَنْهَا May Allah be pleased with her.	رَضِيَ ٱللَّٰهُ عَنْهُمَا May Allah be pleased with them both.	رَحِمَهُمَا ٱللَّٰهُ May Allah bless them both.
عَلَيْهِ ٱلسَّلَامُ May peace be upon him.	عَلَيْهَا ٱلسَّلَامُ May peace be upon her.	عَلَيْهِمَا ٱلسَّلَامُ May peace be upon them both.

Contents

قُل لَّن يُصِيبَنَا إِلَّا
مَا كَتَبَ ٱللَّهُ لَنَا هُوَ مَوْلَىٰنَا
وَعَلَى ٱللَّهِ فَلْيَتَوَكَّلِ ٱلْمُؤْمِنُونَ

Say, "Nothing will ever befall us except what Allah has destined for us. He is our Protector." So in Allah let the believers put their trust.

AL-TAUBAH, 51

Preface

By Dr. Zohair Abdul-Rahman

Believing in the Divine Decree (*al-Qadar*) is considered the 6th pillar of the Islamic worldview that includes belief in Allah, the Angels, the Books, the Messengers and the Last day. The Divine Decree includes belief that Allah has knowledge of all reality—past, present, future, alternative possibilities and that Allah is the only One who brings reality into existence through His Will. This pillar of faith is technically part of belief in Allah, since it is a belief about Allah. It has been singled out as its own pillar demonstrating how important this belief is to our lives. While people may focus on the abstract and philosophical elements of the relation of Divine Will to the human will, the real essence of this pillar lies in understanding its implications for our lives. It is the pillar of faith most commonly invoked in moments of tragedy and hardship. It is called upon in times of anxiety and fear when we confront our trauma. It gives us strength in the darkest and most difficult moments of our life.

Knowing that everything is in Allah's Hands and that He, alone, is in control of every situation is a sobering thought amidst the storms of fears, worries, sadness and depression. Then realizing that the One who is in control is also *Ar-Raḥmān* (The exceedingly Merciful), *Al-Wadūd* (The Most loving),

Al-Ḥakīm (The Most Wise) and *Al-Laṭīf* (The Subtely Kind) grants us hope in the most trying of circumstances. Ibn al-Qayyim (d. 751 AH) explains:

> ***"The past can never be changed or corrected with sadness, but rather with contentment, gratitude, patience and a firm belief in Qadar and the recognition that Allāh decrees whatever He Wills."*** [i]

It is through a firm belief in *Qadar* that we can break free of the shackles of the negative emotions that consume us in the face of adversity. It is a light that illuminates our past and future allowing us to witness the Wisdom and Mercy of Allah in our life and to hope for a better future.

Ibn al-Qayyim says:

> ***"If the veils were lifted from His (Allah's) subtle Kindness and Goodness and what He does for him (the servant) of what he knows and what he doesn't know, his heart would melt out of love for Him, longing to meet Him and he would fall down (prostrating) in gratitude to Him. But instead the hearts are veiled from witnessing this as they persist in the world of desires and focus on the means and so they are prevented from (receiving) his complete blessings. That is the decree of the Mighty and the All-knowing."*** [ii]

---

i Ibn al-Qayyim. *Zād al-Ma'ād,* Vol 2, p. 325.

ii Ibn al-Qayyim. (2019) *Tarīq al-Hijratayn.* Dār Ibn Ḥazm, Beirut. vol. 1, p. 389.

Is it complicated?

Al-Qadar is easy to understand. However, there is a layer that is beyond our human capacity to comprehend. This is not because the concept is irrational, but because our intellects are limited. When our phones cannot capture the brilliance of the night sky, it is not due to a deficiency in the light from the moon, but rather a deficiency in the camera that attempts to capture it. Our minds are the camera and the light from the moon is the light from Divine Decree.

We cannot imagine a cube in 4-dimensions nor can we imagine a colour that we have never seen—but that does not mean they do not have a reality. When it comes to belief in *Qadar*, the relationship between the Will of Allah and the will of the human being is beyond fathoming by our intellect. We are told not to delve into these questions as ultimately it will only yield conjecture and eventually become a means of division.

Abu Huraira reported: The Messenger of Allah ﷺ came to us while we were arguing about the divine decree. Then, the Prophet became angry until his face was red, as if a pomegranate were bursting from his cheeks. The Prophet said, "With this I have commanded you? With this I was sent to you? Verily, the people before you were destroyed when they argued over this matter. I am determined for you not to argue over it." [iii]

iii *Jami' at-Tirmidhī*, 2133.

Outside of this context, it is encouraged to learn about *Qadar*. In fact, one of the narrations that teaches us about *Qadar* was given by the Prophet to a very young companion that wouldn't have been more than 13 years old.

Ibn Abbas reported: I was riding behind the Messenger of Allah, peace and blessings be upon him, when he said to me, "Young man, I will teach you some words. Be mindful of Allah and He will protect you. Be mindful of Allah and you will find Him before you. If you ask, ask Allah. If you seek help, seek help from Allah. Know that if the nations gathered together to benefit you, they could not benefit you unless Allah has decreed it for you. And if the nations gathered together to harm you, they could not harm you unless Allah has decreed it for you. The pens have been lifted and the pages have dried."[iv]

This demonstrates to us the importance of teaching *Qadar* to young children and highlights that it is easy to understand if discussed in the right context.

iv *Jami' at-Tirmidhī*, 2516.

'What does belief in *Qadar* entail?

To appropriately grasp this concept we will highlight the four key principles.

1. Allah knows everything

> ***"Do you not know that Allah knows whatever is in the heaven and the earth? Indeed, that (knowledge) is in a Record. Indeed that, for Allah, is easy."***[v]

The omniscience of Allah is affirmed in several places in the Qurān and Sunnah. His knowledge is written in a record called the *"Lawḥ al-Maḥfūẓ"* (the Preserved Tablet).[vi] There is a ḥadīth that elaborates on this concept,

> ***'Ubadah ibn al-Samit reported: The Prophet ﷺ said, "Verily, the first to be created by Allah was the pen. Allah told it to write, so it wrote all that will exist until forever."***[vii]

Therefore anything that happens in your life, Allah knew it was going to happen before it happened, and it was all written. A common expression that is used is "the pen has dried" referring to the fact that our destiny was written before we were even born.

---

v *al-Hajj*, 22:70

vi *al-Burūj*, 85:22

vii *Jami' al-Tirmidhī*, 3319

2. Allah Wills and Creates everything

"Allah is the Creator of everything" [viii]

"Such is Allah, He does whatever He Wills" [ix]

There are several verses that emphasize that nothing occurs in this world without His permission. Therefore, in addition to Allah knowing everything, He also Wills and Creates everything.

3. Human beings have a will

"So where are you going? This is nothing but a reminder for the worlds. (It is) for whoever among you wills to take the right course." [x]

"Say: The Truth is from your Lord, whoever wills let him believe and whoever wills let them disbelieve." [xi]

Human beings have a will as described in the Qurān. This means that Human beings make choices that they are morally accountable for. This is a reality that is intuitive to every person. We all experience the feeling of a will, choice and making decisions. There is no feeling that we are compelled to act or think in a certain way. Rather, we have the experience of being an individual that thinks, ponders, reflects, chooses and acts.

---

viii *al-Zumar*, 39:62

ix *al-Imrān*, 3:40

x *al-Takwīr*, 81:26–2.8

xi *al-Kahf*, 18:29

4. Human will is Willed by Allah

"And you do not will except if Allah Wills" [xii]

"Allah created you and your actions" [xiii]

Any intentional action has three components: (1) will (2) ability (3) absence of obstacles. Allah creates our will and our capacity along with arranging the affairs of the world that determine the obstacles of the action.

With this in mind, how do we still affirm agency and moral accountability to the human being? The origin of the human will is explained as being a creation of Allah. Hence, everything that we think, choose and act is ultimately created by Him. For any particular action, we are the willful actors and Allāh is the Willful creator, but He is not the actor. Allāh also creates the effects of those actions. So no one can act unless Allah Wills it. Allah is in complete control and could compel us to act in certain ways, but chooses to create our actions in a way that is congruent with what He knows our will would be in each instance. Therefore, we are morally accountable for our actions because they are our actions based on our will.

---

xii *al-Takwīr*, 81:29
xiii *al-Saffāt*, 37:96

This principle cannot be completely grasped with our limited human intellect. The origin of human consciousness, will and desire is a mystery from a neurobiological perspective, let alone a theological one. The philosophy of the mind and attempting to understand where the human will emerges from is a mystery that we will never fully understand. How is it that something metaphysical like thoughts can cause physical changes in our body? How can a thought initiate action potentials in our brains that track down the spinal cord to eventually activate muscles in our limbs? If we cannot understand the interaction of the human will within our own body, then how can we expect to understand the interaction between the Divine will and the human will as its origin?

As Muslims we believe in a human will that makes us responsible for our actions. While we will and perform our actions, we do not create them. We have no control over all the faculties that are required to facilitate a simple action like lifting a hand. We do not create the neurocircuitry, the muscle fibres, the connections that run from our brain to our spine and to our limbs. We have no conscious control over the surge of electrical activity. Our will is not compelled, but it is liberated by the Will of Allah that brings our will to life. Therefore, Allah is the Creator while we are ultimately responsible.

Ibn al-Qayyim says:

"Pre-destination does not nullify actions or result in passivity, but rather it actually inspires exertion and struggle...The servant only achieves what has been destined for him through means (sabab), ability (imkān) and facilitation (hay'). So when the means comes, it connects with the decree that was in the Umm al-Kitāb (Mother of the Book; Preserved Tablets). Every time a person strives hard to attain the means, then what has been decreed comes closer to them. For example, if someone was destined to be the most knowledgeable of His time, then he would never achieve this except through exerting one's self for learning with great passion."

This is why the Prophet ﷺ advised the companions to simply act out their destiny, rather than passively receive their destiny. He said:

"There is none among you, and not a created soul, but has a place either in Paradise or in Hell assigned for him and it is also determined for him whether he will be among the blessed or wretched." A man said, "O Allah's Messenger ﷺ! Should we not depend on what has been written for us and leave the deeds as whoever amongst us is blessed will do the deeds of a blessed person and whoever amongst us will be wretched, will do the deeds of a wretched person?" The Prophet said, "The good deeds are made easy for the blessed, and bad deeds are made easy for the wretched." Then he recited the Verses: "As for him who gives (in charity) and is Allah-fearing And believes in the Best reward from Allah." [xiv]

---

xiv *al-Layl*, 5–6

Our will is not compelled, but it is liberated by the Will of Allah that brings our will to life. Therefore, Allah is the Creator while we are ultimately responsible.

Introduction to *Qadar*

By Dr. Zohair Abdul-Rahman

Our lives are filled with moments that define us. Moments of pure joy that create memories for years to come. But there are also moments of hardship that eat away at our thoughts, relationships, and sometimes even our faith.

It can be hard to sit with the cards we're dealt with. Is my life entirely my own if it's already been written for me? 'Why am I struggling with this hardship, while others have it so easy?', 'Why is this happening? Why now? Why me?' Or, the opposite: 'Why do some people struggle with immense pain, while I am given many blessings?'

Your story doesn't start with your parents, grandparents or even your ancestors. Your story starts with a pen.

سَمِعْتُ رَسُولَ اللَّهِ ﷺ يَقُولُ: إِنَّ أَوَّلَ مَا خَلَقَ اللَّهُ الْقَلَمَ فَقَالَ لَهُ اكْتُبْ.
قَالَ رَبِّ وَمَاذَا أَكْتُبُ قَالَ اكْتُبْ مَقَادِيرَ كُلِّ شَيْءٍ حَتَّى تَقُومَ السَّاعَةُ

Ubādah ibn Ṣāmit said, I heard the Messenger of Allah ﷺ say: "The first thing Allah created was the pen. He said to it: Write! It asked: What should I write, my Lord? He said: Write what was decreed about everything until the Last Hour comes.[xv]

xv *Sunan Abī Dawūd*, 4700

Your story was authored by none other than the Lord of the Worlds, ordained 50,000 years before He created this reality.

عَنْ عَبْدِ اللَّهِ بْنِ عَمْرِو، بْنِ الْعَاصِ قَالَ سَمِعْتُ رَسُولَ اللَّهِ ﷺ يَقُولُ:
كَتَبَ اللَّهُ مَقَادِيرَ الْخَلاَئِقِ قَبْلَ أَنْ يَخْلُقَ السَّمَوَاتِ وَالأَرْضَ
بِخَمْسِينَ أَلْفَ سَنَةٍ–قَالَ: وَعَرْشُهُ عَلَى الْمَاءِ

Abdullah ibn 'Amr said, I heard Allah's Messenger ﷺ say: Allah ordained the measures (of quality) of the creation fifty thousand years before He created the heavens and the earth, as His Throne was upon water.[xvi]

So before existence was even created He knew everything about you. He knew your hopes and dreams, your struggles and trials. He knew your joy and knew your pain. He knew all that you would become and everything you would face in your life.

يَعْلَمُ مَا كَانَ وَمَا سَيَكُونُ، وَمَا لَمْ يَكُنْ لَوْ كَانَ كَيْفَ يَكُونُ

He knows what happened in the past and will happen in the future, as well as that which didn't happen—if it were to ever happen—how it shall happen.

As the scholars have said, Allah knows what was and what is going to be. He even knows what hasn't happened and if it were to happen how it would happen. His knowledge encompasses the enumerable possibilities in this world and how events might have unfolded under different circumstances. There are a near infinite amount of alternate stories and alternate versions of you but he chose to create

xvi *Ṣaḥīḥ Muslim*, 2653

the stories you are witnessing unfold right now and weave it into the fabric of this reality.

Your story started when Allah wrote it down in the heavenly tablets known as the *Lawḥ al-Mahfūzh* (The Preserved Tablets). Ibn Abbās describes these tablets as made from red ruby extending from the Throne of Allah.[xvii] It is also reported from him,

خَلَقَ اللّٰهُ اللَّوْحَ المَحْفُوظَ كَمَسِيرَةِ مِائَةِ عَامٍ، وَقَالَ لِلْقَلَمِ قَبْلَ أَنْ يَخْلُقَ الْخَلْقَ
وَهُوَ عَلَى الْعَرْشِ تَبَارَكَ وَتَعَالَى: اكْتُبْ فقال الْقَلَمُ: وَمَا أَكْتُبُ؟
قَالَ عِلْمِي فِي خَلْقِي إِلَى يَوْمَ تَقُومُ السَّاعَةُ

"Allah created the Lawḥ al-Mahfūzh that (extends) the distance of a 100 year journey. Then He said to the pen before he created the creation: Write My Knowledge of My creation, so it wrote what was to be until the Day of Judgement."[xviii]

Imagine all of the stories of history in one place. The stories of empires and nations, and the stories of the seemingly most insignificant of people with every single moment and emotion recorded. Every single personal story with all of its possibilities.

xvii Tafsīr al-Qurṭubī for Quran, 13:39.
xviii Tafsīr Ibn Kathīr for Quran, 22:70.

'Aṭā' ibn Abī Rabāh said, "In it is (written), 'Fir'awn is from the people of the Fire, and in it is, 'Perish the two hands of Abu Lahab.'"

This tablet contains everyone's unique stories, the precious moments that have been destined before time itself was created. Moments that are strung together in a way only *Al-Ḥakīm* (The Most Wise) could have organized them. In our stories are signs of Allah and His Names that inspire us to draw nearer to Him. Signs of His Wisdom, Justice and Mercy.

فَانظُرْ إِلَىٰ آثَارِ رَحْمَتِ اللَّهِ

"So observe the signs of the Mercy of Allah"[xix]

The story of a young man struggling through poverty and *Ar-Razzaq* enriching him through His bounty is a sign of Divine Mercy (*raḥmah*), Providence (*rizq*) and Favour (*ni'mah*). The story of resistance against tyranny and receiving liberation from *Al-Fattāḥ* (The Opener). The story of redemption as a person overcomes personal demons and finds himself through *At-Tawwāb.* The story of tragedy as a person loses what is so dear to them but finds strength in *Al-Latīf Al-Khabīr.* The story of ambition as a person realizes the seemingly impossible by relying on *Al-Mutawakkil.* The mundane stories of love and affection shared between families that are nothing short of blessings from *Ar-Raḥmān.*

---

xix *al-Rūm*, 30:50

You might say that the test of life is one of perception. Can we recognize the meaning behind the events unfolding before us?

أَلَا لَهُ الْخَلْقُ وَالْأَمْرُ تَبَارَكَ اللَّهُ رَبُّ الْعَالَمِينَ

"To Allah belongs the Creation and the Command"[xx]

He creates you and He creates your stories so you can know Him, love Him and submit to Him.

Our stories have been gifted with existence by the Divine decree, the good of it and the bad. Everyone's story is unique and different. Some are filled with tremendous blessings while others are filled with pain and suffering. Out of all the ways our life could have gone, Allah chooses to create the story that is most appropriate with the nature of the individual and that maximally manifests His Names and Attributes.

This is captured in a weak narration, but its meaning is authentic:

"Allah said, 'Verily, from amongst My slaves is he whose faith cannot be rectified except by being inflicted with poverty, and were I to enrich him, it would surely corrupt him. Verily, from amongst My slaves is he whose faith cannot be rectified except by wealth and affluence, and were I to deprive him, it would surely corrupt him.

xx *al-Aʿrāf*, 7:54

Verily, from amongst My slaves is he whose faith cannot be rectified except by good health, and were I to make him sick, it would surely corrupt him. Verily, from amongst My slaves is he whose faith cannot be rectified except by disease and illness, and were I to make him healthy, it would surely corrupt him. Verily, from amongst My slaves is he who seeks worship by a certain act but I prevent that from him so that self-amazement does not enter his heart. Certainly, I run the affairs of My slaves by My Knowledge of what is in their hearts. Certainly, I am the All-Knower, All-Aware'."[xxi]

xxi Ibn Abi Dunya, *Kitāb al-Awliyā*

1

Where was I before I was born?

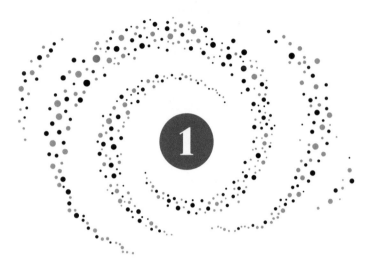

Our lives are defined by pivotal pure moments that define us and shape our identities. It is these precious moments which generate formative memories that will be cherished throughout one's lifetime. At the same time, our lives are scarred with times of hardship and adversity that bruise our conscience, relations, ties of friendship, and our connection with Allah ﷻ. There is no doubt that the objective factors of life can sometimes be debilitating. For, if our lives have already been written and predetermined for us, can we truly say that we own our lives? Why is it that some people go through immense trials and tribulations while I am blessed with the basic comforts of life? Why is it that I experience hardships and difficulties in some areas of my life while others pass by all the stages of their lives and careers with relative ease? The fact of the matter is that the answer to these questions do not stem from your ancestors or your material conditions. Everything, in actual fact, begins with an extraordinary pen.

A pivotal conversation took place at a moment where Heaven, Hell, the Angels, humans, and other created beings did not exist. It was a time when Allah ﷻ alone existed. But this reality would change in a dramatic fashion: in an authentic Hadith, the Prophet ﷺ said that 50,000 years prior to creating the Earth and the Heavens, Allah ﷻ created the Pen. He then issued to it the following imperative:

أُكْتُبْ

"Write."

The Pen said: "What should I write, my Lord?" In response, Allah ﷻ said:

عِلْمِي فِي خَلْقِي إِلَى يَوْمَ تَقُومُ السَّاعَةُ

"[Write down] My knowledge of My creation until the day that the Hour occurs."[1]

---

1 *Sunan Abī Dawūd*, 4700.

This was a critical task, since it meant writing down every single thing decreed until the Last Hour. As such, the Pen wrote and documented every iota of the Divine Decree in *al-Lawḥ al-Maḥfūẓ* (The Preserved Tablet). This special storehouse of knowledge is only accessible to Allah ﷻ, and its exact properties remain unknown. In one interesting report, however, the Companion Ibn ʿAbbās ؓ described this Tablet as consisting of red rubies that descend from the Throne of the Divine.[2] Despite the lack of details concerning the nature of the Tablet, one can know with certainty that it contains the entire history of this universe and the fate of every person to have trekked on this Earth, regardless of whether they are the people of salivation or damnation. It is reported that ʿAṭāʾ ؓ said: "In it is written that Firʿawn (Pharaoh) is from the people of the Fire. Likewise in it is recorded:

تَبَّتْ يَدَا أَبِي لَهَبٍ وَتَبَّ

'May the hands of Abū Lahab perish!'[3]"[4]

However, *al-Lawḥ al-Maḥfūẓ* does not just record the grand and monumental epochs of history. It also contains the mundane and minute particles of individual events, even if they consist of emotions or feelings. Within its pages one can find their own life history neatly arranged and organized in a single chapter, with every small event or feeling put together in a linear and sequential order. This Perfect Book

---

2 *Tafsīr al-Qurṭubī for Qurʾan*, 13:39.

3 *al-Lahab*, 111:1.

4 *Sunan al-Tirmidhī*, 2155.

is a reflection of Allah's infinite Wisdom, for, after all, He is *al-Ḥakīm* (the Most Wise). Through this perfect arrangement, one realizes the Mercy and Greatness of his Lord, a theme reflected in the following verse:

فَٱنظُرْ إِلَىٰٓ ءَاثَٰرِ رَحْمَتِ ٱللَّهِ

"See then the impact of Allah's Mercy."[5]

This is an important imperative since Allah ﷻ programmed every one of us with the intimate perception of Him even before we were brought into existence in this world. This innate awareness and appreciation of His presence was decreed so that we may recognize our Lord, revere Him, and submit to Him.

But where were we before we entered this world? Essentially, our present bodily and spiritual being in this world lies between two metaphysical planes: 1) *'Ālam al-Dharr*, which refers to the realm of pre-existence that marked our origins, and 2) *'Ālam al-Barzakh*, which is the realm that we will inhabit in our graves. It is not hard to notice that both of these realms are characterized by a horrifying darkness and coldness. The only way that they can be illuminated is through the mechanism of Allah's benevolent Decree to His servant and the commission of numerous good deeds.

5 *al-Rūm*, 30:50.

A covenant was made after Allah عز وجل directly asked every human soul, "Am I not your Lord?" This explains why humans have the natural tendency to believe in a Creator, though they may choose to not submit to this innate inclination.

It is reported that the Prophet ﷺ said:

إِنَّ اللَّهَ خَلَقَ خَلْقَهُ فِي ظُلْمَةٍ

"Allah created His creation in complete darkness."[6]

The same theme is underscored in one of the moving events that occurred in the realm of pre-existence, regarding which Allah ﷻ states:

وَإِذْ أَخَذَ رَبُّكَ مِن بَنِي آدَمَ مِن ظُهُورِهِمْ ذُرِّيَّتَهُمْ

"And when your Lord brought forth from the loins of the children of Adam their descendants."[7]

This is a vivid scene where all the descendants of our father Adam ﷺ will be presented to him, protruding from his back. According to the Prophet ﷺ, in this momentous event, a batch of his offspring were displayed before Adam ﷺ, and Allah ﷻ said to him: "I have created these for Paradise, and they are going to do the deeds of those who go to Paradise." And then Allah ﷻ will once more take a group of Adam's children and descendants from his back and say: "I have created these for the Hellfire, and they are going to do the deeds of those who go to Hell."

This was a momentous metaphysical event, where the lines of every family tree stood before their Lord from the highest ancestor to the lowest descendent, with these groupings

---

6 *Sunan al-Tirmidhī*, 2642.

7 *al-A'rāf*, 7:172.

of people appearing like *dharr* (little particles). Every one of us was present in this plane throughout the Valley of Naʿmān, which is found in ʿArafah.[8] During the Hajj season, this location is filled to the brim with millions of Muslims per annum. But in this pre-creation setting, all of humanity—consisting of every person from the beginning of creation until the Last Day—was present in this single plane of ʿArafah. This explains why in linguistic terms, the term ʿArafah refers to knowing or recognizing one's Lord, since it signifies the very location where the original covenant of monotheism was made and is renewed every time it is visited. This covenant was made after Allah ﷻ directly asked every son of Adam ﷺ the following question:

أَلَسْتُ بِرَبِّكُمْ

"Am I not your Lord?"[9]

This is the first direct conversation that every human had with their Lord. While it may be forgotten in express terms, it remains deeply imprinted and embedded at the spiritual level. This explains why humans have the natural tendency to believing in a Creator, though they may choose to not submit to this innate inclination.

Yet another powerful observation that can be made with this episode is that it commences with the query, "Am I not your Lord?" This is very similar to the question that every deceased

---

8 *Musnad Imām Aḥmad*, 2455.

9 *al-Aʿrāf*, 7:172.

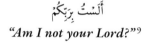

person will have to address when they enter their grave. Describing this pre-creation episode further, the Prophet ﷺ said: "Allah cast His light upon the creation and whoever was touched by that light is guided. And whoever was not goes astray." In another version of this Hadith, the Prophet ﷺ said:

وَجَعَلَ بَيْنَ عَيْنَيْ كُلِّ إِنسَانٍ مِنْهُمْ وَبِيصًا مِّن نُّورٍ

"Then Allah placed between the eyes of every person among them a portion of light."

However, this light did not exist at a consistent level and intensity among all individuals, just like the brightness of people in their graves and on the Day of Judgement. Amazed by this spectacle, Adam ﷺ began to trek and observe the variations of light among his progeny, admiring the illuminated members of his progeny. As the Prophet ﷺ noted, he eventually set his sights on one particular person who was exuding an intensely bright and dazzling light. It was quite clear that this person would be a figure distinguished with many acts of worship. In fact, this person had an outstanding profile: he would be a Prophet living a life of gratitude and pray to Allah every last third of the night and fast every other day. Adam ﷺ addressed his Lord, saying:

أَيْ رَبِّ! مَنْ هَذَا؟

"O my Lord! Who is this?"

Allah ﷻ said: "This is your son Dāwūd." Adam ﷺ then said: "How many years does he have?" Allah ﷻ replied: "He will live for 60 years." Adam ﷷ then made the following request: "Give him 40 of my years so that he may live longer."[10] It is possible that Adam ﷷ walked through this gathering, met your soul, and found your amount of good deeds to be remarkable.

During this mass summit, the souls of humans will meet and interact with one another as well. The Prophet ﷺ is confirmed to have said:

اَلْأَرْوَاحُ جُنُودٌ مُجَنَّدَةٌ

"The souls of a similar likeness
are like conscripted soldiers."[11]

Due to their intense light, the souls of the believers will resemble one another and have a natural affinity to one another. Thus, they will be able to recognize their counterparts with relative ease. For instance, it is confirmed in an authentic Hadith that the Prophet ﷺ said that the *wuḍū'* of the believers and their good deeds will shine on their bodies.[12] This light will be so intense that according to the Companion Ibn Masʿūd رضي الله عنه, if a believing soul were to come across a group of 100 souls and 99 of them were hypocrites with one believer, they would be able to recognize the latter due to their intense light.[13]

---

10 *Sunan al-Tirmidhī,* 3076.

11 *Ṣaḥīḥ al-Bukhārī,* 3109.

12 *Ṣaḥīḥ al-Bukhārī,* 136.

13 Ibn Baṭṭah, *al-Ibānah al-Kubrā* (Riyadh: Dār ar-Rāyah, 1994), vol. 2, p. 455.

A person's standing in this world, their station in the Afterlife, and who they will accompany in the next world, has already been predestined. The Prophet ﷺ said:

جَفَّ الْقَلَمُ عَلَى عِلْمِ اللهِ

"The pens have dried with the Knowledge of Allah."[14]

Despite this being the case, can it be possible for some aspects of the Divine Decree to be amenable to change? The answer is a yes, since there are multiple layers of the Decree. The key document in this regard is *al-Lawḥ al-Maḥfūẓ*, which is permanent and unchangeable. But at the same time, there are certain days or special events in which Allah ﷻ allows His slave to make adjustments to His destiny. For instance, there is the special night of *Laylah al-Qadr,* which occurs once per year. Likewise, when a person is inside their mother's womb, they were subject to special provisions of the Divine Decree. A person can alter certain realities of their fate through the initiative of making *duʿā'* (supplication) and good deeds. With His perfect knowledge, Allah ﷻ already is aware of these forthcoming alterations, and has recorded them in *al-Lawḥ al-Maḥfūẓ*. He already knows what will change and has taken them all into consideration in the Perfect Record.

With full certainty, there is no doubt that a person's fate has been written and registered. This might cause a person to question what is the benefit of doing goods if they are already

14 *Sunan al-Tirmidhī*, 2642.

assigned with a fixed end. In fact, the Companions asked the Prophet ﷺ the very same question, with the latter replying:

إِعْمَلُوا فَكُلٌّ مُيَسَّرٌ لِمَا خُلِقَ لَهُ

"Do [your good deeds] for everyone will be facilitated with what they were created for."[15]

A person attains salvation on the Day of Judgement through their own deeds and acts, not what has been written through Allah's Foreknowledge. He has full knowledge of every person's fate, but they must live through it and decide to pursue it through their personal choices, which will ultimately make them deserving of their destination. In other words, the life trajectory that Allah ﷻ assigns for a person is due to His knowledge that this individual would choose such a lifestyle himself. As a person proceeds through their life and sees the chapters of their destiny unfold, they will come to the realization that Allah ﷻ truly knows best.

15 *Ṣaḥīḥ Muslim*, 2647.

Allah ﷻ has full knowledge of every person's fate, but they must live through it and decide to pursue it through their personal choices, which will ultimately make them deserving of their final destination.

2

Why did Allah choose this time for me?

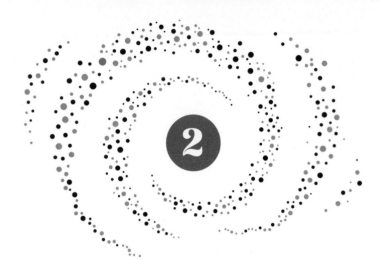

Allah ﷻ wrote all of the various possibilities of your life trajectory in *al-Lawḥ al-Maḥfūẓ*, with only one of them actually being realized during your short stay in this Earth. You might prove to be the saviour of a particular family member or person in this generation, or you might be the response to a *duʿā'* (supplication) that one of your forefathers made decades or centuries ago, wishing for someone down the family line to achieve a desired goal or objective. Allah's Knowledge is perfect; He chose you to arrive at this particular generation and setting, whereby you may leave a meaningful legacy after living your life to its decreed end. Regardless of the exact factors that may have defined your existence, there can be no doubt that your very being was perfectly planned by Allah ﷻ, with your familial, environmental, and social factors being catered to your personality and lifelong goals.

Always try to perceive yourself as being a shimmering light from Allah's Decree that was conceived in the perfect moment. It is likely that you are the extension of a light that was shone by an ancestor or senior figure who came before you. Recall how—as discussed in the previous chapter—Adam ﵇ was able to witness his entire progeny in the special plane of pre-creation. It is possible that he witnessed your light and was amazed by the legacy that you will leave behind. Similarly, when the Prophet ﷺ ascended up to the highest point of the universe during the remarkable al-Isrā' wa al-Miʿrāj journey, the entirety of his Ummah was presented to him. He was able to witness all his followers in this auspicious setting, and was impressed by the shimmering light reflected by many members of the Muslim community.

Every person has certain dreams, with the same rule holding true for previous dreams. The stark reality is that many of our dreams might not be realized for ourselves, but it is possible for them to be achieved by the generations to come. For instance, Ibrāhīm ﵇ dreamed of having a descendent who would preach the message of monotheism in the land of Mecca, but it would take thousands of years for this desire to be realized with the birth of the Prophet Muhammad ﷺ.

In other cases, the dream is achieved in a closer timeframe. For instance, after witnessing a pleasant dream one night, ʿUmar ibn al-Khaṭṭāb ﷺ appeared with a wide smile on his face and said: "Who is this child from my descendants who will fill the Earth with justice after it has been filled with injustice?" Just a few years later, his great-grandson ʿUmar ibn ʿAbd al-ʿAzīz ﷺ would be born and restore a strong moral character to the Umayyad Empire. It is quite possible that Malcolm X—who assumed the Islamic name El-Hajj Malik El-Shabazz—constituted the divine response to a *duʿā'* made by an oppressed and enslaved woman in the United States. The key question is whether we have the potential and capacity to cultivate a blessed presence regardless of our setting or circumstances. When the Prophet ʿĪsā ﷺ was born, he said:

وَجَعَلَنِي مُبَارَكًا أَيْنَ مَا كُنتُ

"He [Allah] has made me a blessing wherever I go."[16]

The Quranic exegetes explained this verse by noting that it meant that ʿĪsā ﷺ brought goodness to any environment or setting that he inhabited. But this ruling is not exclusive to him. In actual fact, if we emulate the behaviour and actions of the pious, we too can be blessed regardless of our place or location in this plant. A person's birth may even be a blessing by bringing goodness and happiness to their family, or it may be the materialization of another figure's *duʿā'* centuries prior.

---

16 *Maryam*, 19:31.

When we arrive in this world, we almost instantly become attached to certain hopes and ambitions that often impose pressure and stress on us. This problem is often compounded with varying levels of darkness that frustrate us at every juncture. Such problems may include a dysfunctional household, the treachery caused by someone else, or oppression from a dominant figure hovering above us. The Prophet ﷺ called injustice and oppression *ẓulumāt*, that is, various levels of darkness. But this can be countered through a variety of means. Allah ﷻ minimizes the darkness of the world through His revelation and His Divine Decree, both of which bring light to the creation. However, there is another way that he illuminates the world: through your deeds. In fact, some scholars have said that these sources of light are alluded to in the following verse:

نُّورٌ عَلَىٰ نُورٍ

"Light upon light."[17]

Each one of us has the latent potential to activate a light within us. Such a move is in fact necessary, lest we ourselves become manifestations of darkness. If that occurs, then the darkness of the world will engulf us as well, with the darkness in turn becoming multilayered.

[17] *al-Nūr*, 24:35.

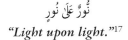

This very theme is touched in the following verse:

ظُلُمَاتٌ بَعْضُهَا فَوْقَ بَعْضٍ

"Or [their deeds are] like the darkness in a deep sea, covered by waves upon waves." [18]

When plunged in such a state, the state of darkness is so severe that one will not even be able to see their own hands. But the ultimate choice is yours: in your finite time in this planet, you can choose to either be a blessing or a curse in your era. This is in fact the moral lesson that the Prophet ﷺ was alluding to when he said:

فِيْ كُلِّ قَرْنٍ مِنْ أُمَّتِيْ سَابِقُوْنَ

"In every generation of my Ummah, there are forerunners." [19]

As a scholar noted, to be among those stars of a given generation, one must become what is known as *ibn al-waqt*, or the child of the moment.

Unlike the atomistic and individualistic worldview that dominates the current worldly setting, our lives are actually interconnected and tied to one another. Our stories converge throughout time and space in a myriad of ways. Your parents

---

[18] *al-Nūr*, 24:40.

[19] Abū Nuʿaym, *Ḥilyah al-Awliyāʾ wa Ṭabaqāt al-Aṣfiyāʾ* (Cairo: Maṭbaʿah al-Saʿādah, 1974), vol. 1, p. 8.

may have had to undergo a number of costly and risky pregnancies before they could finally conceive you and bring you to this world, since Allah ﷻ knew that this was your perfect moment, where you would leave a meaningful mark for humanity. You might be living in a certain town because a Muslim centuries prior passed by your same district and asked Allah for one of His slaves to be born there and serve His faith. Your existence may be the result of millions of oppressed people praying to Allah for a reformer and saviour to come and bring them deliverance on this Earth. The Prophet ﷺ is reported to have said:

هَلْ تُنْصَرُونَ وَتُرْزَقُونَ إِلَّا بِضُعَفَائِكُمْ

"Are you given victory or sustenance except by how you treat your vulnerable ones?"[20]

In this report, the Prophet ﷺ is stressing an important indicator of worldly success: being a blessing to another person is sometimes the reason for which one's decree is blessed. Regarding himself, the Prophet ﷺ said:

دَعْوَةُ أَبِي إِبْرَاهِيمَ، وَبُشْرَى عِيسَى بِي

"[I am] the prayer of my father Ibrāhīm, and the glad tidings of ʿĪsā."[21]

---

20 *Ṣaḥīḥ al-Bukhārī*, 2896.

21 *Musnad Imām Aḥmad*, 22361.

Despite being conceived in the darkest of eras, the birth of the Prophet ﷺ engulfed the world with light and marked a new beginning. Shortly before he was born, his mother saw a light that illuminated the palaces of the Levant. This signified that his mercy would illuminate the world in its entirety.

But what about your own self? What did Allah ﷻ choose for you by causing you to exist in this very moment? The one who denies such a divine wisdom is only displaying their manifest ignorance in the matter. In one of his aphorisms, Ibn 'Aṭā' Allāh al-Iskandarī رحمه الله said:

مَا تَرَكَ مِنَ الْجَهْلِ شَيْئاً مَنْ اَرَادَ اَنْ يَحْدُثَ
فِيْ الْوَقْتِ غَيْرُمَا اَظْهَرَهُ اللّٰهُ فِيْهِ

"The one who wants to appear in a moment other than what Allah has manifested is full of ignorance."

Know and appreciate the fact that Allah ﷻ wants the best for you, appreciate your purpose in the spatio-temporal setting you find yourself in, and then make the most out of that moment. It is often the case that individuals read about past epochs and periods and wonder why they could not be born during that age. It is interesting to note that the Successors (Tābiʿūn) felt this very way when they met and corresponded with the Companions (Ṣaḥābah), for they wished to live with the blessed Prophet ﷺ and support the Islamic message with his guidance. But the Companions reminded them of the extreme hardships and adversities that they had to face while supporting Islam. They also warned them that had they lived in that age, there is no guarantee that they would have embraced the Islamic message; it is possible that they would have sided with the polytheists and fought under the banner of Abū Jahl![22] There is no guarantee that they would have been moved by the message of the Qur'an and accepted Islam at the hands of the Prophet ﷺ. The same question can be posed for the previous eras with other Prophets. For instance, during the age of Nūḥ ﷷ, one may have sided with the majority of his people who rejected his call of monotheism, thereby falling into disbelief. Likewise, with respect to the call of Mūsā ﷷ, it is possible that one would side with the evil troops of Pharaoh instead of the Prophet of Allah ﷻ. We can learn from these past stories and apply them to our present setting. In our current world, there are evil groups led by modern Pharaohs who we must oppose with the words of truth revealed by our Creator. Take the best stand that you can within your present circumstances and ensure that you emulate the model of the pious and righteous. Before you were born, Allah ﷻ knew what was best for you, and He precisely set your time and location in this planet. Take that fact into account and ensure that you make the best out of your circumstances to improve yourself and the world that you inhabit.

---

22 *Musnad Imām Aḥmad*, 24311.

3

What happened on my birth day?

You entered this world in a cold, unclothed, confused, and vulnerable state. Despite these early limitations, Allah ﷻ provided you immediate moral and physical support through your caregivers, who provided you comfort with their warm hands, nourished you with milk, and ensured that your body could grow despite the dangers around you. Allah ﷻ ensured that you were allotted your sustenance even before your birth, and prior to your helpless existence.

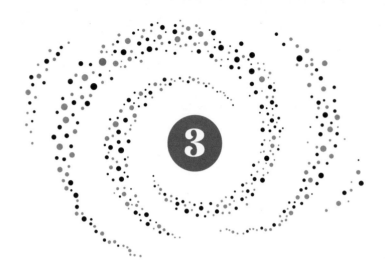

The Creator reminds humanity of these blessings in the following series of verses:

قُتِلَ الْإِنسَانُ مَا أَكْفَرَهُ مِنْ أَيِّ شَيْءٍ خَلَقَهُ مِن نُّطْفَةٍ خَلَقَهُ فَقَدَّرَهُ ثُمَّ السَّبِيلَ يَسَّرَهُ

"Condemned are humans! How ungrateful they are! From what substance did He create them? He created them from a sperm-drop, and ordained their development. Then He makes the way easy for them."[23]

According to exegetes of the Qur'an, "Then He makes the way easy for them" can refer to either the miraculous path out of the womb or the path of spiritual guidance that He facilitated you with. These interpretations are not mutually exclusive. For if a person fails to appreciate the Mercy of his Lord during the process of birth, then how can he possibly recognize his Lord as his Creator and Sustainer? Undoubtedly, the episode of birth is one of Allah's greatest marvels and wonders, which ultimately allows us to appreciate His Mercy and submit to Him in praise.

The miraculous nature of giving birth has been reiterated in a number of stories in the Qur'an. For instance, after being unable to conceive a child for numerous decades and reaching an old age, Allah ﷻ blessed Sārah with Isḥāq ﷺ. Similarly, after remaining fatherless for all his life and reaching the final stages of his life, Zakariyyā ﷺ was given Yaḥyā ﷺ. But perhaps the most miraculous and inspiring story is that of

23 *'Abasa*, 80:17–20.

Every day and every penny that a person will earn in this world was already decreed for them by Allah's command when they were still a fetus inside their mother's womb.

Maryam, who give birth to ʿĪsā ﷺ despite her pure chastity and being a virgin. But every single birth in and of itself is a miracle, for Allah ﷻ allows a new human to sprout from the darkest and most desolate of places. Allah ﷻ has alluded to this fact in the following verse:

يُخْرِجُ الْحَيَّ مِنَ الْمَيِّتِ وَيُخْرِجُ الْمَيِّتَ مِنَ الْحَيِّ

"He brings forth the living from the dead and the dead from the living."[24]

Even before you are born, the protection that was granted to you throughout your nine-month stay in your mother's womb is a miracle in and of itself. For throughout that lengthy stay, Allah ﷻ ensured that the womb was a place of safety, calm, and nourishment, for, as He states:

ثُمَّ جَعَلْنَاهُ نُطْفَةً فِي قَرَارٍ مَكِينٍ

"Then [We] placed each [human] as a sperm-drop in a secure place."[25]

Just like in the case of our womb, Allah ﷻ assured humanity that their stay in this Earth will be guaranteed with a minimum degree of security and provision. In one key verse, He states:

وَلَكُمْ فِي ٱلْأَرْضِ مُسْتَقَرٌّ وَمَتَاعٌ إِلَىٰ حِينٍ

"You will find in the earth a residence and provision for your appointed stay."[26]

---

[24] *al-Rūm*, 30:19.

[25] *al-Mu'minūn*, 23:13.

[26] *al-Baqarah*, 2:36.

Interestingly, just like in the case of the womb, Allah uses the same trilateral root of *qāf-rā'-rā'* to describe the Earth. This indicates that just like the safety and security that we feel while in the womb of our mother, in the Earth Allah provides us a secure settlement and ensures that our basic needs and desires are met. If he happens to lose something, Allah replaces it with something better. This point was beautifully illustrated by Ibn al-Qayyim ﵀, who said that the believer should reflect on the foetus when it is situated in the womb. During its time there, it receives its nourishment only from a single pathway, which is the umbilical cord. Once they enter the world, this cord is permanently disconnected from them. But they then receive something better than that: two pathways of milk. And once the young child is weaned off, they lose access to those two pathways. But Allah ﷻ recomposes them with four sources of nourishment, with every one of them being superior to their mother's milk: 1) the meat of animals, 2) the nutrient-rich crops of the Earth, 3) fresh and sweet water from the Earth's rivers, and 4) the rich array of dairy products produced from the milk of cows, sheep, and goats. When the believer dies, they will be blocked from these four pathways. But they will then receive the greatest recompense, as the eight gates of Jannah will be opened for them. Ibn al-Qayyim ﵀ concluded his discussion by stating: "And if a path of *rizq* is blocked by His Wisdom, know that He will open for you from His Mercy a path even more beneficial for you."[27] From this previous point, we learn

[27] Ibn al-Qayyim, *al-Fawā'id* (Riyadh: Dār 'Aṭā'āt al-'Ilm, 2019), p. 79.

that if a source or form of divine provision is blocked, it is solely from Allah's Wisdom.

Your life's major hallmarks and achievements were already pre-determined when you were still inside the womb of your mother. In a pivotal Hadith, the Prophet ﷺ said: "Allah has appointed a special Angel as the caretaker of the womb, and he would say [to Allah]: 'My Lord, it is now a drop of fluid, my Lord, it is now a clot, my Lord, it has now become a lump of flesh.' And then once Allah decrees to give it its final form, the Angel says, 'My Lord, is it male or female? My Lord, is it evil or righteous? My Lord, how many years will it live? My Lord, how much sustenance have You prescribed for it?'"[28] Allah ﷻ will then provide the Angel answers for every one of these questions, which will be recorded when the fetus is still in the womb of the mother. The repercussions of this pre-birth decree are astounding. It means that every day and every penny that a person will earn in this world was already decreed for them when they were in their mother's womb.

The Companion Abū al-Dardā' رضي الله عنه adds an additional layer of information to this account. He notes that on the 40th night after conception, a Divine Decree is issued with respect to the foetus's appearance, character, lifespan, and sustenance on a green scroll which hangs from the Throne of the Almighty. Just like in the case of *al-Lawḥ al-Maḥfūẓ* (The Preserved Tablet), this constitutes a permanent record of what legacy

---

28 *Ṣaḥīḥ al-Bukhārī*, 6595.

you will leave on this planet. And as your decree is being carried out, the scroll in question ages and its page begins to deteriorate. Once your appointed time on the Earth expires, the scroll falls from the Throne.[29]

Imagine that your life has just begun, and you are still in the beginning section of your scroll. The first chapter is just about to commence. The *du'ā'* (supplication), words of *dhikr* (remembrance), and silent hopes of all those who came prior to you had an effect on how and when you appeared in this transient world. The moment you enter the external universe, Shayṭān poked you, the Angels surrounded you with their wings, your parents viewed you with limitless pleasure, and Allah ﷻ graced you with His gaze. In this setting, you are crying and confused with your new environment that is unlike the setting you had been accustomed to, while your parents and family members are overjoyed to welcome you into their home. The *adhān* (call of prayer) is called into your ear, which serves two moral purposes. First, it awakens the innate recognition of Allah ﷻ that lies latent within the depths of the soul. But as a second matter, it also underscores the importance of *ṣalāh* (prayer) for the believer, as it comprises their spiritual nourishment in this world and the Hereafter. Likewise, the special *taḥnīk* ceremony performed with a date provides the newborn baby basic nourishment and serves as a reminder that a person in this world must

29 Ibn Baṭṭah, *al-Ibānah al-Kubrā* (Riyadh: Dār al-Rāyah li al-Nashr wa Tawzī', 2005), vol. 4, p. 226.

live through moderation and be satisfied with a modest and non-extravagant living.[30] This was in fact the mode of living championed by the Prophet ﷺ, regarding whom his beloved wife ʿĀ'ishah said:

تُوُفِّيَ النَّبِيِّ صَلَّى اللّٰهُ عَلَيْهِ وَ سَلَّمَ حِيْنَ شَبِعْنَا مِنْ أَسْوَدَيْنِ: أَلتَّمَرُ وَ الْمَاءُ

"The Prophet ﷺ passed away from this world when we would satisfy our hunger with just the two black things: dates and water."[31]

The process of *taḥnīk* in actuality symbolizes this very standard of living, since it is performed by chewing a date and then feeding it to the newborn infant. The date is thus mixed with saliva, which in essence constitutes a date and water. The same moral lesson is also reiterated in other rulings informed by the Shariah, such as circumcising a newborn boy[32] and shaving their head on the seventh day[33]; then the latter's equivalent weight in gold is given away as *ṣadaqah* (charity). Both of these acts symbolize the importance of being content with what is necessary and stripping away anything that is excessive or unnecessary. Just like these two latter rituals, there is the blessed *ʿaqīqah* practice, where one sacrifices an animal on behalf of the newborn and distributes its meat among one's family and members of the community.

---

30 See *Ṣaḥīḥ Muslim*, 2145.

31 *Ṣaḥīḥ al-Bukhārī*, 5383.

32 *Ṣaḥīḥ al-Bukhārī*, 5550.

33 *Sunan al-Tirmidhī*, 1522.

The distributed food serves as a reminder that the child does not deprive the parents from their wealth and savings; instead, it enriches their *rizq* (provision). This same theme is underscored in the following Quranic verse:

وَلَا تَقْتُلُوا أَوْلَادَكُم مِّنْ إِمْلَاقٍ نَّحْنُ نَرْزُقُكُمْ وَإِيَّاهُمْ

"Do not kill your children for fear of poverty. We provide for them and for you." [34]

Ibn ʿAṭāʾallāh al-Iskandarī ﷺ also said:

أَنْعَمَ عَلَيْكَ بِالْإِيجَادِ أَوَّلًا وَ ثَانِياً بِتَوَالِي الْإِمْدَادِ

"And He bestowed His blessings upon you, first by bringing you into existence, and second, through uninterrupted sustenance."

The benefits found in the *ʿaqīqah* are not just restricted to this temporal world. As the scholars note, it will serve as a means for the child to intercede for its parents on the Day of Judgement and ensure their salvation in the Hereafter. This source of goodness is stored in the name of the child even before they perform any act of good in this world.

The Islamic topic of sacrifices confers a number of other teachings as well. For example, consider the story of Ibrāhīm and Ismāʿīl ﷺ, when Allah ﷻ ordered the father to sacrifice his son. When Ibrāhīm ﷺ was just about to carry out the

---

[34] *al-Anʿām*, 6:151.

sacred order, Allah ﷻ sent down a ram and ordered him to kill it instead. This marked an astounding blessing, as Ismāʿīl ﷺ was saved, and subsequently another nation was born. Every one of our births also marks a celebration as well. According to Ibn al-Qayyim, the event of a new Muslim being born is also celebrated by the Prophet ﷺ, since it increases his Ummah in its number.[35]

Every person has a special role to undertake in this Ummah. This explains why the right to a virtuous name holds a special bearing in Islam, since it enacts an effect on the person. It is thus important to name one's children after the heroes of the faith. For instance, Ṭalḥah ؓ used to name his children after the Prophets. Similarly, Zubayr ؓ used to name his children after the brave *shuhadāʾ* (martyrs) of the Ummah. The Prophet personally urged Muslim parents to name their children noble titles like ʿAbdullāh and ʿAbd al-Raḥmān. Muslims girls should be given names of a similar quality, such as Maryam, Khadījah, and Fāṭimah. The most important factor is to ensure that one's children are named after people of quality and noble individuals that they can emulate.

Thanks to the Divine Decree of Allah ﷻ, you can and will become a force of good in this world. That assurance does not come from the hospital doctors or your parents, but from Allah ﷻ Himself.

---

35 Ibn al-Qayyim, *Tuḥfah al-Mawlūd,* p. 100.

On this point, one may reflect on the following verse:

كُلَّ إِنسَانٍ أَلْزَمْنَاهُ طَائِرَهُ فِي عُنُقِهِ

"We have bound every human's destiny to their neck."[36]

According to the great commentator Mujāhid ﵀, the verse denotes the following:

مَا مِنْ مَوْلُوْدٍ إِلَّا فِيْ عُنُقِهِ وَرَقَة مكتوبٌ فِيْهَا شَقِيٌّ أَوْ سَعِيْدٌ

"No one is born except that on his neck is a scroll which has been evil or good inscribed on it."[37]

While it is true that a person's surroundings and environment matter, the fact remains that a person can turn any environment into a means of elevation. You are blessed with a family who will in some shape or form shape how you become, but the ultimate trajectory that you take in your life lies in your hands.

36 *al-Isrā'*, 17:13.

37 *Tafsīr al-Qurṭubī for Qur'an*, 17:13.

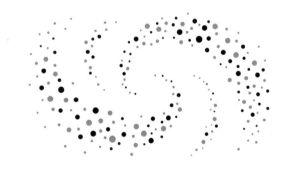

The du'ā', words of dhikr, and silent hopes of all those who came before you had an effect on how and when you appeared in this transient world.

4

Why is this my family?

Your family may be a great blessing or a great test, but in either case, you are forever linked to them biologically and emotionally. The stories, life experiences, and memories that you create with them will last you for your entire life. Is there a hidden wisdom embedded within this reality, and what lessons can one derive from it? The answer for these queries can be found in the Qur'an, which emphasizes the sacrifices that parents make for their children.

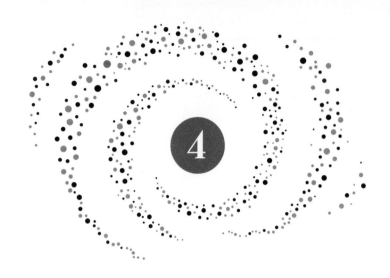

Many of these sacrifices cannot be appreciated until one becomes a parent themselves. It is for this very reason that Allah ﷻ says:

وَوَصَّيْنَا ٱلْإِنسَٰنَ بِوَٰلِدَيْهِ إِحْسَٰنًاۖ حَمَلَتْهُ أُمُّهُۥ كُرْهًا وَوَضَعَتْهُ كُرْهًاۖ
وَحَمْلُهُۥ وَفِصَٰلُهُۥ ثَلَٰثُونَ شَهْرًاۚ حَتَّىٰٓ إِذَا بَلَغَ أَشُدَّهُۥ وَبَلَغَ أَرْبَعِينَ سَنَةً قَالَ رَبِّ
أَوْزِعْنِيٓ أَنْ أَشْكُرَ نِعْمَتَكَ ٱلَّتِيٓ أَنْعَمْتَ عَلَيَّ وَعَلَىٰ وَٰلِدَيَّ وَأَنْ أَعْمَلَ صَٰلِحًا
تَرْضَىٰهُ وَأَصْلِحْ لِي فِي ذُرِّيَّتِيٓۖ إِنِّي تُبْتُ إِلَيْكَ وَإِنِّي مِنَ ٱلْمُسْلِمِينَ

"We have commanded people to honour their parents. Their mothers bore them in hardship and delivered them in hardship. Their bearing and weaning is thirty months. In time, when the child reaches their prime at the age of forty, they pray, 'My Lord! Inspire me to be thankful for Your favours which You blessed me and my parents with, and to do good deeds that please You. And instil righteousness in my offspring. I truly repent to You, and I truly submit [to Your Will].'"[38]

Through this verse, we derive the core teaching that we must honour our parents for their sacrifices. But not every person has such a stable and comfortable upbringing, whereby they enjoy a preferable degree of positive parental influence. For instance, the Prophet Mūsā ﷺ was raised and brought up in the palace of Firʿawn, who was one of the most brutal and bloodthirsty tyrants in history. But he received much comfort thanks to the presence of Āsiyah, who—despite being the wife of Firʿawn—was a selfless and gentle believer. It is likely

38 *al-Aḥqāf*, 46:15.

the case that many children living in the palace of a tyrant like the Egyptian Pharaoh would have emulated his path and opt to become an oppressor. But Mūsā 🙼 shunned the doors of narcissism and oppression, instead embracing the altruistic model set by Āsiyah.

In a similar fashion, Ibrāhīm 🙼 was tested with a harsh and abusive father, who would—besides expelling him from his home—eventually have him thrown into a roaring fire.[39] Despite these bitter adversities, Ibrāhīm 🙼 himself would become a caring and loving father to his children.[40] In fact, there are a number of scholars who states that Ibrāhīm's name is actually the fusion of the word Ab (father) and Raḥīm (merciful), which translates to "a merciful father". Although the veracity of this interpretation is contentious, there is no doubt that Ibrāhīm 🙼 possesses the title of Abū al-Anbiyā' (Father of the Prophets). From the story of Ibrāhīm 🙼 we derive the lesson that on some occasions a child can contrarily respond to the abuse meted by their parents, such that they become loving and merciful parents.

This reciprocal response, however, does not develop in a smooth fashion. In this regard, one may consider the story of 'Umar ibn al-Khaṭṭāb 🙼. As historians mention, 'Umar 🙼 had a harsh and abusive father, and for this reason, the former hated the latter. But because he had become accustomed

---

[39] *Maryam*, 19:46.

[40] *al-Tawbah*, 9:114.

to this abusive relationship, ʿUmar ﷺ himself was likely to follow the same path with his own children. But the message of Islam completely changed this trajectory, as ʿUmar ﷺ was able to reorient his path and pursue the moral guidance and justice found in his newfound faith. Thanks to this paradigmatic shift in his lifestyle, ʿUmar ﷺ would become an exemplary father. In fact, the degree that ʿAbdullāh ibn ʿUmar ﷺ loved his father was just as intense as the degree that ʿUmar ﷺ hated his own father al-Khaṭṭāb. Ironically, the morally detrimental father al-Khaṭṭāb would actually end up raising a son who would become one of the greatest fathers in history, such that his son ʿAbdullāh ﷺ would follow his path of goodness.

Two of the four believing women who perfected their faith consisted of a mother and daughter. The first was the Queen of the Heart of the Prophet and the Mother of the Believers Khadījah bint Khuwaylid ﷺ, while the second was the leader of the female believers in Paradise, Fāṭimah bint Muhammad ﷺ. The latter was the mother of the leaders of the youths of Paradise, namely al-Ḥasan and al-Ḥusayn ﷺ, who both manifested the values of bravery, chivalry, and leadership during the most difficult time period of the Muslim Ummah. Undoubtedly, they absorbed these fathers from their valiant father, ʿAlī ibn Abī Ṭālib ﷺ, who stood and supported the call of Islam during its nascent period as a youth.

Though we may be inclined to deem our childhood to be difficult and traumatic, we should not fail to also acknowledge the positive experiences during our upbringing and the love and care we received from our parents during our vulnerable moments.

At the same time, you must be mindful of the fact that your parents had their own parents as well, and they oftentimes made decisions in light of the experiences they had in the past. It is very possible that they had to undo some of the harsh elements that they had previously internalized from their own parents, so that they could give you the treatment and love they aspired to receive during their own childhood. Similarly, your grandparents may find in you an opportunity to display more affection and care than what they did to their own children. Even more interestingly, it is possible that your parents had varying experiences in their respective childhoods, but were still able to converge and unite through the marriage with the facilitation of Allah ﷻ.

The stage of childhood can be described as a second womb, wherein our temperaments and personalities are fashioned through a mixture of positive and negative experiences within our family setting. Though we may sometimes be inclined to deem our childhood to be difficult and traumatic, we should never fail to acknowledge the positive experiences that we had during our upbringing and the love and care we received from our parents during our vulnerable moments. There is no such thing as a perfect and ideal parent, and for this reason it is imperative to acknowledge the limitations of our guardians and caregivers without any malice or ill regard. This is because while it is true that your parents comprise the greatest form of influence in your life, you still function as an autonomous being with your own traits and qualities. As such, you can and should be able to absorb the positive characteristics of your parents without being hampered by their negative traits. You should be able to lead a lifestyle that is defined by qualities loved and promoted by Allah ﷻ, starting with the ones that you witnessed in the conduct of your parents.

Even if you happened to never have a parent with such qualities, bear in mind that we comprise an Ummah that is led by a blessed orphan; the Prophet ﷺ leads all the members of his nation just like a father leads his children. It is authentically narrated that he said:

إِنَّمَا أَنَا لَكُمْ بِمَنْزِلَةِ الْوَالِدِ أُعَلِّمُكُمْ

"I am to you like a father whereby I teach you."[41]

The Prophet ﷺ, his pure family, and his noble Companions ﷺ are the best of examples for our moral conduct and golden standards in this world. In our day-to-day affairs, we should also aim to have companions that emulate those aforementioned standards to the best degree possible.

In his aphorisms, Ibn ʿAṭāʾallāh al-Iskandarī ﷺ said:

لَا تَصْحَبْ مَنْ لَا يُنْهِضُكَ حَالُهُ وَلَا يَدُلُّكَ عَلَى اللَّهِ مَا قَالُهُ

"Do not keep company with anyone whose state does not inspire you, and whose speech does not lead you to Allah."

41 *Sunan Abī Dāwūd*, 8.

It is quite possibly the case that with respect to your parents, you may have a myriad of beautiful memories that you cannot recall anymore, despite them being deeply implanted in your soul. They may only exist as the faintest of flashbacks and recollections in your mind. You may see a past picture of you and your family and only vaguely recall the background events that defined its occurrence. Regardless of all the hardships and difficulties that you went through in your childhood, you went through a series of defining moments that shaped your character and identity today. It is thus necessary for you to celebrate your childhood in its entirety as a means to spiritually rejuvenate yourself.

قل لن يصيبنا إلا
ما كتب الله لنا هو مولىنا
وعلى الله فليتوكل المؤمنون

Say, "Nothing will ever befall us except what Allah has destined for us. He is our Protector." So in Allah let the believers put their trust.

AL-TAUBAH, 51

5

What shaped my personality?

By their intrinsic nature, children vary in their behavioural patterns and temperaments. Parents recognize this reality best, and can almost instinctively identify differences between them from the start. Some are loud and brimming with external energy, some are shy and composed, while others lie somewhere in between. Allah ﷻ has allotted every one of us a myriad of different traits and qualities, which have implications for our spiritual and mental endurance. But ultimately, how we cultivate these talents and endowments is in our hands.

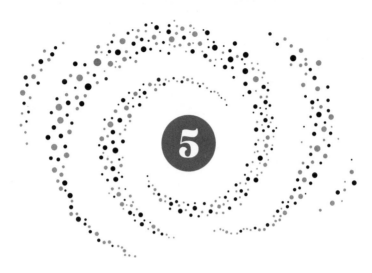

The question of how much control we actually exert in this matter can be derived from the following verse:

كُلٌّ يَعْمَلُ عَلَىٰ شَاكِلَتِهِ

"Everyone acts in their own way."[42]

Every human being is born and shaped in light of the nature that Allah ﷻ has decreed for them. And as they grow, their positions and stances are shaped by their first impressions and experiences. For example, the first time that you enter a *masjid* has a momentous effect on whether you develop an affinity to the house of Allah ﷻ and feel inclined to visit again. If you were received well by the congregants, greeted with smiles, and felt comfortable with the group praying around you, you will likely desire to go and visit there again. But if you felt that you were being given a cold reception and people were disturbing you during your prayers and litanies, then you may not wish to enter that particular location anymore. Even the very act of prayer can be viewed in varying lights depending on how one was introduced to it during their childhood. If one's parents taught them the act of worship in a positive light whereby its importance and blessings were underscored, they will be determined to perform it in a regular basis. But if they were introduced to prayer as if it was a burden of meaningless movements that one was forced to undertake without any explanation or rationale, then they will likely view it in a negative light.

---

42 *al-Isrāʾ*, 17:84.

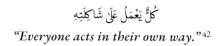

Parents are oftentimes the first outlet through which a person identifies with the markers of Islam, such as giving charity to the poor and needy, praying together, and the blessings found in eating together, particular in the month of Ramadan. For instance, it is related that 'Abdullāh ibn 'Umar ﵄ would not consume a meal in his residence unless if there was an orphan at the table as well. In his rationale in doing so, Ibn 'Umar ﵄ mentioned that this was a trait that he acquired from his father, who stressed the importance of feeding orphans.

But some behavioural traits are not externally induced. Instead, they are innate to a person's own natural disposition. For instance, some children are extroverted and enjoy to partake in activities with others. Other children, however, are introverts, and as such they love to indulge in private activities. In a similar fashion, while some children are able to maintain a disciplined demeanour in their day-to-day activities, others may have behavioural issues, which prevent them from following orders in an automatic fashion, although they love to emulate their parents without the need for any external stimulus. But it is not only the positive elements of parenthood that bear a deep effect in our mental and spiritual being. Negative behaviour traits—such as argumentation and hot tempers—are often absorbed by children from their parents, who openly display such traits. Constantly witnessing one's parents engage in fights and disputes can cause someone to feel helpless and weak, which may, in the future, result in the formation of a deferential attitude.

But how much of your personality was developed through your own self and disposition? The most balanced answer for this boiling question is that an individual's personality is a product of both nature and nurture. From this personality, one develops their *akhlāq* (character), which is their general behavioural traits in the public and private spheres. Scholars note that one should visualize the realm of personality like a number of seeds that lie latently under the soil. What causes them to sprout and grow is the light of revelation and the radiance of faith, both of which squarely lie within the control of the individual self. By carefully watering and nourishing these seeds, a person can grow and develop into a morally upright person. The failure to do so will result into the growth of evils and vices.

These aforementioned points can be derived and appreciated from the story of a notable Companion by the name of Ashajj ʿAbd al-Qays ﷺ, who was a tribe leader. When his tribe went to visit the Prophet ﷺ, they travelled in remarkable haste, as they were excited to see the leader of the Islamic faith in person. But Ashajj ﷺ quite surprisingly tarried; this was a deliberate move, as he sought to ensure that all the logistics and preparations for his tribe's journey were complete. When he finally arrived in Medina and visited the Prophet ﷺ, he was not rebuked for his delay.

In fact, the Prophet ﷺ clearly observed the positive dimensions in his deferral, and praised him by stating:

إِنَّ فِيكَ خَصْلَتَيْنِ يُحِبُّهُمُ اللَّهُ الْحِلْمُ وَالْأَنَاءُ

"Verily, you have two qualities that Allah loves: your ḥilm (forbearance) and anā' (patience)."[43]

Ashajj was praised because he fused two different yet complementary traits. At first sight, they might be dismissed as being traits of a weak leader, but upon reflection they are indicators of strength and strategic calculation. He exercised tolerance and easy-going behaviour with his people, but at the same time he made careful and strategic projections for his tribe by ensuring that everything was in order for his people.

In another narration, the Prophet ﷺ mentioned the qualities of *ḥilm* and *ḥayā'* (modesty). Once again, modesty and shyness may at first sight seem to be a weak trait, but is actually a strength, since it pushes one to refrain from sinful and shameless conduct.

Ashajj was amazed to hear this positive appraisal from the Prophet ﷺ, and said: "O Messenger of Allah, did I acquire these traits, or did Allah create these traits within me?" The Prophet ﷺ responded by stating: "Rather, Allah put them in you." In other words, he was alluding to the fact that Ashajj was created with these traits. Ashajj was most pleased to hear this and responded by stating:

---

43 *Sunan Abī Dāwūd*, 5225.

الحمدُ للهِ الَّذي جبَلَني على خُلقَينِ يُحِبُّهما اللهُ

"All praise be to Allah Who shaped me with two qualities that He loves."[44]

From this report, a key point of benefit can be derived. The traits that Ashajj was given were divinely-planted as seeds from the point of birth. Allah ﷻ then guided and inspired Ashajj to then draw these latent qualities in his outward conduct, thereby becoming part of his personality.

It is true that forbearance, patience, and modesty are easily activated if a person is already possessive of an introverted disposition. But if someone is an extrovert, they can still attain the fruits of Allah's guidance if they sincerely strive in His path. This is why Allah ﷻ states:

وَٱلَّذِينَ جَاهَدُواْ فِينَا لَنَهۡدِيَنَّهُمۡ سُبُلَنَا

"As for those who struggle in Our cause, We will surely guide them along Our Way."[45]

Echoing this same theme, the Prophet ﷺ is reported to have said:

إِنَّمَا العِلْمُ بِالْتَعَلُّمِ وَإِنَّمَا الحِلْمُ بِالْتَحَلُّمِ

"Knowledge is only acquired by seeking knowledge and forbearance is only attained by exercising forbearance."[46]

44 *Sunan Abī Dāwūd*, 5225.

45 *al-ʿAnkabūt*, 29:69.

46 al-Muttaqī al-Hindī, *Kanz al-ʿUmmāl fī Sunan al-Aqwāl wa al-Afʿāl* (Beirut: Mu'assasah al-Risālah, 1405/1985),vol. 10, p. 347.

Every human being is born and shaped in light of the nature that Allah عَزَّ وَجَلَّ has decreed for them. And as they grow, their positions and stances are shaped by their first impressions and experiences.

The same rule can be applied for unlearning bad habits, such as restraining one's temper. While the latter is a relatively more difficult process, it can still be exercised and learned by a person. Just as one can learn a good quality, they can likewise unlearn a bad one. In fact, with regard to the latter the reward is actually greater since one must exert greater efforts to attain that station. In his book on aphorisms, Ibn 'Aṭā'allāh al-Iskandarī ﷺ said:

حُسْنُ الْأَعْمَالِ نَتَائِجُ حَسَنِ الْأَحْوَالِ وَحُسْنُ الْأَحْوَالِ
مِنْ نَتَائِجِ التَّحَقُّقِ فِيْ مَقَامَاتِ الْإِنْزَالِ

"Good deeds result from good states, and good states arise from the stations wherein those who have spiritual realizations abide."

Every person should aim to capitalize on the potential good qualities that they have and strive to make them their dominant personality traits. By doing so, they will be able to obtain the pleasure and happiness of Allah ﷻ. This is possible if someone accompanies pious friends and companions in this world, and tries to emulate their praiseworthy traits to the best degree possible. When good and pious minds come together, multiple paths of righteousness can be erected, whereby everyone can expand their horizon of ethical conduct and safely undertake their journey to Allah ﷻ.

6

Why do I have these (dis)abilities?

Every one of us has strengths and weakness. Likewise, while we all have the strength to undertake a myriad of ends, the fact remains that many of us face objective limitations in this world, such as disabilities. Unquestionably, there is no doubt that good health and well-being is the greatest blessing after having faith in Allah ﷻ.[47] After all, the former gives us certain privileges, such as mobility, prowess, and work opportunities in a myriad of sectors. But what if that were not the case, and Allah ﷻ decreed to strip you of

---

[47] *Musnad Imām Aḥmad*, 10.

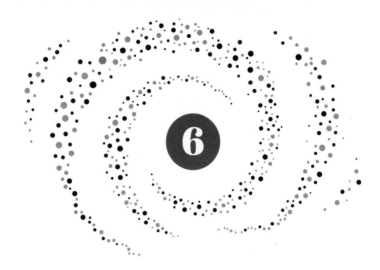

some of these faculties? You may lack strength, mobility, or some mental capabilities. If this is the case, one should not give up hope, for there are blessings embedded in disabilities and illnesses. It may be that Allah ﷻ wishes to grant that affected person and their loved ones a special blessing in this world and the Hereafter.

In fact, while it is true that the Prophet ﷺ said that there is no greater blessing than *'āfiyah* (sound well-being), he also urged members of his Ummah to never curse an illness, even if it was a fever. For as he ﷺ said, "Do not curse any illness, even a fever, because it burns off your sins."[48] The rationale for this morale injunction is that Allah ﷻ is present with the one who is ill, with 70,000 Angels also travelling and visiting the affected person to shower their blessings. A similar degree of reward and divine pleasure is extended to the caregiver and patient family members of the sick person as well, since they are also tested with this burden in their day-to-day activities, where they may in some cases face this test for multiple years. Despite its negative features, such an affliction provides the entire family a chance to solidify their faith and realize growth in their religious conviction and character. Undoubtedly, witnessing one's loved one face physical or cognitive constraints can be a terrifying and damaging ordeal for the entire family, but it serves as a spiritual reminder of the fragility of humans and how everyone will someday return to Allah ﷻ. A sincere Muslim who sees a loved family member fading and gradually leaving this world submits to

[48] *Sunan Ibn Mājah*, 3649.

Allah's Divine Decree and realizes that every event of this world has a higher purpose or wisdom. Allah ﷻ may be using this healthy relative as a means to ensure the faith and moral confidence of this affected family member or to help the disabled at the community level. By exhibiting patience and acceptance of the Will of their Creator, this caregiver and helper can earn their express ticket to Paradise.

It is related that after returning from a journey, the noble Successor 'Urwah ibn al-Zubayr ﷺ was informed that his favourite son Muhammad had a serious fall from a high location and subsequently died. Instead of weeping or becoming shocked, 'Urwah ﷺ said: "O Allah, all praise is due to You. To Allah we belong, and to Him shall we return. He gave me seven children and He only took one." Later on in his life, 'Urwah's leg was afflicted with a deadly infection, and it had to be amputated. Despite losing his leg, 'Urwah ﷺ said: "All praise is due to Allah. I had four of my full limbs (i.e. my two arms and my two legs), and Allah only took one of them." He proceeded to recite the following *du'ā'* (supplication):

رَبِّ لَئِنْ كُنْتَ قَدْ اَخَذْتَ فَلَقَدْ اَعْطَيْتَ وَ لَئِنْ كُنْتَ قَدْ ابْتَلَيْتَ فَقَدْ عَافَيْتَ

"O my Lord, where You have taken from me, You have still left more to remain. And where You have put me in a trial, You still granted me health."[49]

[49] Ibn Kathīr, *al-Bidāyah wa al-Nihāyah* (Beirut: Dār al-Kutub al-'Ilmiyyah, 2015), vol. 5, p. 111.

Imam al-Zuhrī ﵀ noted that on the same night that his foot was amputated, ʿUrwah ibn al-Zubayr ﵀ still recited his portion of the Qur'an during the *qiyām* (special night) prayer. One can even find modern examples of this God-consciousness as well. For instance, the famous and beautiful man of Gaza and exemplar of patience known as Khaled Nabhan (who poetically called his killed granddaughter the "soul of my soul") recently counselled a girl who had lost her war due to the 2023-2024 Israeli genocide by saying: "Do not worry, my loved one, your leg has already gone to Paradise." The stark reality is that sometimes we learn to fly when our worldly wings are clipped. Paradoxically, it is during times of grief and disability that we actually become the most spiritually upright and elevated in rank. The truly disabled people are those whose hearts are deaf, dumb and blind. It is related that when Ibn ʿAbbās ﵄ went blind in the later stages of his life, he said:

إِن يَأْخُذِ اللَّهُ مِن عَينَيَّ نورَهُما فَفي لِساني وَسَمْعِي مِنهُما نورُ

"If Allah removes the light from my eyes,
my tongue and my ears make up
for them in light."[50]

In a similar manner, it was once said to Qatādah ﵀: "Why are the blind so much deeper than those who can see?"

---

50 Ibn Qutaybah, *ʿUyūn al-Akhbār,* vol. 4, p. 57.

Qatādah ﷺ responded by saying:

لِأَنَّ أَبْصَارَهُمْ تَحَوَّلَتْ إِلَى قُلُوبِهِمْ

*"Because their vision was turned
inwards into their hearts."*

The Prophet ﷺ guaranteed Uthmān ibn ʿAffān ﷺ Paradise
due to all the wealth that he spent in the cause of Allah.
But in the Sunnah corpus one also finds a report where the
Prophet ﷺ promised a woman Paradise because she opted
to exercise patience with her frequent seizures. Throughout
his life the Prophet ﷺ honoured disabled and physically
defective people, a factor that indicates their elevated station
in the sight of Allah ﷻ. For instance, in the nascent Muslim
community, the Prophet ﷺ appointed ʿAbdullāh ibn
Maktūm ﷺ—who was blind—as the *muʾadhdhin* (caller)
of the Medina Mosque. Other honourable people from his
community include Nusaybah ﷺ, who lost her arm in the
Battle of Yamāmah, Abdullāh ibn Masʿūd ﷺ, who was
extremely short and usually took a bow-legged posture, and
Abū ʿUbaydah ﷺ lost all of his teeth and developed a lisp
due to him pulling the helmet from the blessed face of the
Prophet ﷺ during the Battle of Uḥud. Our communities
should also emulate the prophetic model by having disabled
people in prominent roles.

Allah ﷻ gently corrected the Prophet ﷺ due to him frowning at a blind man. In light of this divine instruction, the Prophet ﷺ admonished his community by stating: "Do not stare at a person with leprosy or a skin condition in a way that would make them feel despised." A woman suffering from a mental illness came to the Prophet ﷺ and requested him to help her fulfill a task. The Prophet ﷺ respectfully called her by her name and said: "Choose whichever road you would like and I will come with you and fulfil whatever you need."

A community that is truly inspired by the prophetic ethos is one which recognizes the various strengths and limitations that they have, while being united with the goal of growing together such that no member is left behind. There is no doubt that the sincere Muslim who faces a mental challenge or disability in this world will be handsomely reimbursed in the Hereafter, but this does not mean that they should simply be left to suffer in this world. Instead, they should always feel welcomed in the Muslim community and be given any possible opportunities to participate and undertake good deeds, for a believer feels immense pain if they ever fail to seize a good opportunity to perform a pious act. The Companions رضي الله عنهم were undoubtedly the golden standard in this regard, but in some circumstances, even they were unable to perform the optimal level of actions that they desired. For instance, a group of young Companions رضي الله عنهم requested to participate in the Battles of Badr and Uḥud, but they were turned away because they had not reached the age of adulthood and thus lacked the physicality and stamina to be in the battlefield. Another group of the Companions ﷺ were also heartbroken when they were unable to participate in the Battle of Tabūk. The Qur'an vividly illustrates the grief that they experienced in the following verse:

تَوَلَّوا۟ وَّأَعْيُنُهُمْ تَفِيضُ مِنَ ٱلدَّمْعِ حَزَنًا أَلَّا يَجِدُوا۟ مَا يُنفِقُونَ

"They left with eyes overflowing with tears out of grief that they had nothing to contribute."[51]

Today, we find individuals who are unable to fast because they are diabetic or they are unable to perform the *sujūd* (prostration) in prayer because they suffer from a back problem. Allah ﷻ showers these individuals with His Mercy by allotting them special concessions and alternative acts of worship that they may perform, while also assuring them that they will receive the same reward.

In the Islamic ethos, physical abilities have little value, since the true yardstick of ethical value is having sound intentions. In fact, individuals who are stronger or intellectually gifted may actually be more likely to fall into the dangerous spell of arrogance, which destroys a person's good deeds in entirety. Some of the most intelligent and powerful people in this world ended up rejecting Allah ﷻ and His religion due to their arrogance, such as Qārūn, who falsely alleged that he earned all his wealth thanks to his own knowledge.

51 *al-Tawbah*, 9:92.

By asserting such a false claim, he become a fool who failed to recognize the fact that these bounties were gifts given to him by his Creator.

The paradox of this world is that having gaps and disadvantages in this domain actually cause you to be more humble and have a heart that is predisposed to attaining the pleasure of Allah ﷻ. Even if you may feel behind in a certain area or milestone in this life, know that Allah has given you a head start in your other-worldly ranking. No matter what disadvantages you may have, strive to search for the avenues to please your Creator and you will find a plethora of successful avenues. Ibn ʿAṭāʾallāh al-Iskandarī رحمه الله said:

أَنْوَارٌ أُذِنَ لَهَا فِي الْوُصُولِ وَ أَنْوَارٌ أُذِنَ لَهَا فِي الدُّخُولِ

"There are lights that are allowed to arrive, and then there are lights that are allowed to enter."

7

Why do I look like this?

In this temporal world, much emphasis is given on looks and appearances, such that we may even have a sense of low self-esteem if we feel that we are unattractive or physically lacking. When we compare ourselves to others, we often come to the conclusion that we lack the beauty, attractiveness, charisma, and charm of our peers. But have you ever considered the possibility that beauty may actually be a curse, and not a blessing? You can and should come to the realization that renouncing the standards of beauty imposed by the world can liberate you from the delusions and false promises of the Devil.

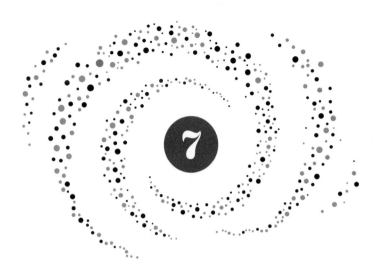

We do sometimes need a friend or loved one to give us a confidence booster and reassure us of our worth. During the time of the Prophet ﷺ, there was a Companion of Bedouin origins by the name of Ẓāhir رضي الله عنه. Due to his not-so-pleasant appearance, he faced some major self-confidence issues and believed that he lacked any worth in society. Whenever he went to visit the city of Medina, he would go to the Prophet ﷺ and present him a modest present, out of the hope that he would be noticed. The Prophet ﷺ would always demonstrate to Ẓāhir that he had his undivided attention, and would ensure to raise his spirits in a lighthearted manner. On one occasion, the Prophet ﷺ grabbed Ẓāhir from behind in the marketplace and began to playfully wrestle with him and shout: "Who is going to buy this one from me? Who is going to buy this one from me?" Despite being amused by this joke, Ẓāhir said: "O Messenger of Allah, who would want to buy me anyway?" At this point, the Prophet ﷺ could have continued laughing but he was well-aware that Ẓāhir was experiencing low self-esteem issues due to his appearance. Consequently, the Prophet ﷺ turned towards Ẓāhir and said to him:

وَلٰكِنَّكَ عِنْدَ اللهِ غَالٍ

"But you are priceless in the sight of Allah." [52]

Through this statement, the Prophet ﷺ was demonstrating the fact that true beauty lies in one's upright and morally virtuous character. In other words, the way that the Creator ﷻ sees you

52 *Musnad Imām Aḥmad*, 12560.

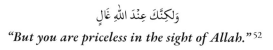

Our Lord—Who holds the beautiful attribute and name of al-Muṣawwir—has also provided each one of us what we need to succeed in this life. One should never suppose that the outwardly beautiful person is "complete" or perfect.

is how you should view yourself as well. Every person's appearance is perfectly in line with how their Creator ﷻ sought it to be:

ٱلَّذِى خَلَقَكَ فَسَوَّاكَ فَعَدَلَكَ فِىٓ أَىِّ صُورَةٍ مَّا شَآءَ رَكَّبَكَ

"[What has emboldened you against your Lord, the Most Generous] Who created you, fashioned you, and perfected your design, moulding you in whatever form He willed?"[53]

One of Allah's sublime names is al-Muṣawwir (The Bestower of Forms), which refers to His perfect capacity to give every one of His servants a unique and beautiful *ṣūrah* (form). Notwithstanding this fact, the Prophet ﷺ said:

إنَّ اللَّهَ لَا يَنْظُرُ إلى صُوَرِكُمْ وأَمْوالِكُمْ، ولَكِنْ يَنْظُرُ إلى قُلُوبِكُمْ وأَعْمالِكُمْ

"Allah does not look at your bodies and wealth. Rather, He looks at your heart and deeds."[54]

In addition, Allah ﷻ warns us to not be deluded by the trappings found in outward and superficial beauty. For example, when speaking of the hypocrites, He exposes their debased inward nature:

وَإِذَا رَأَيْتَهُمْ تُعْجِبُكَ أَجْسَامُهُمْ وَإِنْ يَقُولُوا تَسْمَعْ لِقَوْلِهِمْ كَأَنَّهُمْ خُشُبٌ مُسَنَّدَة

"When you see them, their appearance impresses you. And when they speak, you listen to their speech. But they are like planks of wood leaned [against a wall]."[55]

---

[53] *al-Infiṭār*, 82:7–8.

[54] *Ṣaḥīḥ Muslim*, 2564.

[55] *al-Munāfiqūn*, 63:4.

In his commentary on this verse, Imam al-Ṭabarī ﷺ said in his book of Quranic exegesis:

وَإِنَّمَا هُمْ صُوَرٌ بِلَا أَحْلَامٍ

"They are just like empty forms without purpose."[56]

In other words, the hypocrites are individuals who are completely devoid of any inner spirit or God-consciousness. Despite their outward form being pleasant, they are spiritually bankrupt people. Individuals of such a disposition oftentimes aim to seek the validation of others on social media platforms by sharing their images and expecting words of praise and approval from their peers. The believer avoids such baseless endeavours, for they are well aware that every single oddity or defect in their body holds a latent purpose. When Uways al-Qarnī ﷺ asked Allah ﷻ to cure him from leprosy, the Prophet ﷺ said: "O Allah, leave the size of a coin." This was requested so Uways ﷺ could always see the mark of this disease and maintain his humility. From this report, one derives the spiritual lesson that being obsessed with having a "perfect" appearance is inversely related with God-consciousness and moral conduct.

Our Lord—Who holds the beautiful attribute and name of al-Muṣawwir—has given every one of us what we need to succeed in this life. One should never suppose that the

---

56 *Tafsīr al-Ṭabarī for Qur'an*, 63:4.

outwardly beautiful person is "complete" or perfect, as illustrated in the story of Qārūn. Then there are individuals who are outwardly unattractive but internally beautiful, such as Ẓāhir ﷺ. But then there is a supreme category of individuals who are beautiful in both the external and internal dimensions, such as the Prophet ﷺ, whose beauty surpassed the luminescence and splendour of the shining Moon.[57] Added to this category is the Prophet Yūsuf ﷺ, who was given half of beauty.[58] Notwithstanding this last category, it is important to note that neither the Prophet ﷺ nor Yūsuf ﷺ earned their value through their physical appearance. However, their beautiful presence attracted their audiences to the message of monotheism that they were tasked to propagate. In other words, beauty can be effectively used as a variable of goodness and to promote the truth. A prime example of this is the Companion ʿAbdullāh ibn ʿAbbās ﷺ. Observers around him said that if one looked at him, they would immediately assume that he was from the most beautiful of people. And when he spoke, they would immediately assume that he was from the most intelligent of people.[59]

When a person rises in their level of God-consciousness, they begin to disregard beauty standards and instead devote all their time and wealth to obtain the pleasure of their Creator.

---

57 *Sunan al-Tirmidhī*, 3636.

58 *Ṣaḥīḥ Muslim*, 162.

59 al-Dhahabī, *Siyar Aʿlām an-Nubalāʾ*, vol. 2, p. 352.

A prime example of this is the Companion Muṣʿab ibn ʿUmayr ﷺ, who was considered the most handsome and elegant bachelor of Mecca. In the pre-Islamic era, he was famed for his youth, beauty, and wealth. But after accepting Islam, he no longer paid any attention to these standards and lived a life of poverty. In fact, when he was martyred, he was covered in the dirt of the battlefield with his unwashed wounds, and there was no garment available to cover his entire body. This sight was so depressing that some of the Companions would cry whenever his martyrdom was mentioned, as they would recall his fragile state before being buried. But if one carefully reflects on the life of Muṣʿab ibn ʿUmayr ﷺ, they will realize that he abandoned all the transient standards of beauty and instead trekked the permanent path of righteousness, which preserved his life and example in this world among the members of the Ummah, such that Muslim children continue to be named after him.

Righteous deeds can become a person's true garment of beauty. This explains why ʿUthmān ibn ʿAffān ﷺ once said: "Whenever a person does an action, Allah clothes him with that deed." Should the deed be sound and sincere, then the garment will likewise be proper. But if the deed is evil, then the garment will likewise be wicked. How a person behaves in the sight of their Creator is how they will behave and act in the presence of the creation.

In this regard, Ibn ʿAbbās ﷺ said:

إِنَّ لِلْحَسَنَةِ ضِيَاءً فِي الْوَجْهِ وَنُورًا فِي الْقَلْبِ وَقُوَّةً فِي الْبَدَنِ وَسَعَةً فِي الرِّزْقِ وَمَحَبَّةً فِي قُلُوبِ الْخَلْقِ

"Good deeds bring beauty to the face, light to the heart, strength to the body, abundance to one's wealth, and love in the hearts of the creation."[60]

Upon careful observation, it becomes abundantly clear that these are the same outwardly pleasant dimensions that people pursue in this world. The statement of Ibn ʿAbbās ﷺ clarifies that these prizes are only found through sincerity and exercising virtuous behaviour, not falling into vice and vanity. For sins distort the face and lead to the destruction of one's provision. Of course, even the believer sins, but through Allah's Mercy their wrongs are covered; their outward beauty only exists due to Allah's veil over them. In this regard, Ibn ʿAṭā'allāh al-Iskandarī ﷺ said:

مَنْ أَكْرَمَكَ فَإِنَّمَا أَكْرَمَ فِيكَ جَمِيلَ سِتْرِهِ فَالْحَمْدُ لِمَنْ سَتَرَكَ لَيْسَ الْحَمْدُ لِمَنْ أَكْرَمَكَ وَ شَكَرَكَ

"Whoever honours you, only does so due to the beauty of His veil upon you. Therefore, praise is to Him Who veiled you, not to the one who praises you."[61]

---

60 Ibn al-Qayyim, *al-Dā' wa al-Dawā'*, p. 135; Ibn al-Qayyim, *Rawḍah al-Muḥibbīn*, p. 586.

61 Ibn *ʿAṭā'allāh al-Iskandarī, al-Ḥikam*, p. 22.

This explains why the Prophet would regularly make the following invocation:

اللَّهُمَّ كَمَا حَسَّنْتَ خَلْقِي فَحَسِّنْ خُلُقِي

"O Allah, as You have beautified my appearance, then beautify my character."[62]

Through this supplication, one is asking Allah ﷻ for inner beauty just as He has made one's outward complexion and form beautiful. They are pleased with how Allah ﷻ has fashioned them, and instead focus on the internal elements of character and sincerity, which truly constitute their beauty. And because this worldly life is full of trials, it is often the case that many people will be unable to realize the beauty of their character until they undergo the harshest of tribulations.

قُل لَّن يُصِيبَنَا إِلَّا مَا كَتَبَ ٱللَّهُ لَنَا هُوَ مَوْلَىٰنَا وَعَلَى ٱللَّهِ فَلْيَتَوَكَّلِ ٱلْمُؤْمِنُونَ

Say, "Nothing will ever befall us except what Allah has destined for us. He is our Protector." So in Allah let the believers put their trust.

AL-TAUBAH, 51

---

62 *Ṣaḥīḥ Ibn Ḥibbān*, 959.

When a person rises in their level of God-consciousness, they begin to disregard beauty standards and instead devote all their time and wealth to obtain the pleasure of their Creator.

8

Why am I rich or poor?

Facing financial difficulties can be a devastating experience, as one naturally feels that the pillars of support that they erected for their family are at the verge of collapsing. Frustration at one's plight sometimes causes one to pose questions, such as whether others are well-off because they work harder and if it is one's own fault for their lack of financial success. Is it possible to understand and appreciate the blessings embedded in *rizq* (provision) even if we are personally financially hampered? The answer is in the affirmative, for everything can be appreciated through a single truth: Allah ﷻ has already decreed every penny and cent that you will earn in this life, and you should exercise full trust and dependence on His Decree.

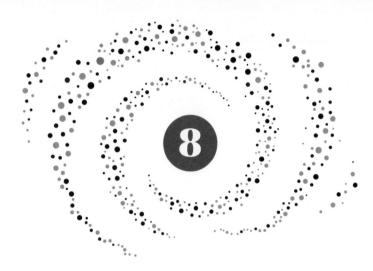

The loss of wealth can be a terrifying ordeal for a person, since a person must be impacted by the feelings of fear, anxiety, regret, shame, and uncertainty for the future. A person might be fearful to speak of their dire state to their loved ones and family; no one is comfortable of speaking of their failure to their dependants, as it affects their standing and dignity and also causes one's loved ones to feel hurt and abandoned.

Financial problems almost inevitably create tensions in the household, with a series of stressors affecting both the parents and children. However, even in the most difficult of financial difficulties, there are spiritual and moral lessons that can be learned. Embedded in such trials are potential faith-affirming or faith-affirming hurdles; whether one will leave from such trials in a stronger or weaker state depends on their perseverance and determination. In order to overcome these challenges in a God-conscious manner, one must emulate the teachings of the past Prophets ﷺ. For instance, Prophet Ayyūb ﷺ was severely tested for several years in his life by being deprived of his family, health, and wealth. Nevertheless, he exercised beautiful patience throughout his ordeal and was immensely rewarded by his Lord. Likewise, after calling to the message of Islam, the Prophet Muhammad ﷺ was subject to a crippling boycott on the part of the polytheists, which led to the less of all his possessions and the death of his beloved wife Khadījah bint Khuwaylid ﷺ and his uncle Abū Ṭālib.

Being content with one's level of *rizq* is pivotal to having a good opinion of Allah and being able to move forward in one's life.

'Abdullāh ibn Mas'ūd ﷺ is reported to have once said:

حَبَّذَا الْمَكْرُوهَانِ الْمَوْتُ وَالْفَقْرُ

"Accept two things that you dislike: death and poverty."

He also added: "By Allah, I do not care whether Allah tests me with wealth or poverty, for the right of Allah in each of them must be fulfilled. So if it is wealth, then the answer is gratitude and if it is poverty, then the answer is patience."[63] In a similar fashion, Sufyān al-Thawrī ﷺ once said: "True richness is only found in contentment." Our own blessed Prophet is reported to have said: "If Allah wills good for a servant, He puts richness in his soul." The meaning of this prophetic tradition is that such a blessed servant will be content regardless of what he has and is given, even if he faces dire straits in his day-to-life. In other words, the truly God-conscious servant will be content regardless of his circumstances, and he will always feel that he is rich.

Material deprivation is something that Allah's faithful servant should welcome in this world, as it is a signpost of Allah's pleasure and contentment with them. The Prophet said: "If you only knew the rewards that you had with Allah, you would want to be increased in poverty and need."

63 'Abdullāh ibn al-Mubārak, *al-Zuhd wa al-Raqā'iq*, p. 566.

Yet, the Prophet ﷺ was not requesting members of his Ummah to ask Allah ﷻ for the circumstance of poverty per se. Rather, he was urging them to ask the Creator to confer them the rank of the poor and their blessed lens of the world. For the poor are people of contentment, suffice with a little, avoid the trappings of wealth, and seek the Hereafter. This is the type of mentality which every believer should aim to internalize if they wish to enter Paradise in a relatively fast pace. Imam Ḥasan al-Baṣrī ﵀ once said:

مَنْ رَضِيَ مِنَ اللهِ بِالْيَسِيْرِ مِنَ الرِّزْقِ رَضِيَ اللهُ مِنْهُ بِالْقَلِيْلِ مِنَ الْعَمَلِ

"Whoever is pleased with Allah with a little amount of sustenance, Allah will be pleased with a little bit of his deeds."

This is in fact the state of the majority of the Ummah: they are impoverished individuals who frequently engage in *dhikr* (remembrance) of the Divine, maintain their daily obligations, and sleep in a state of full contentment, even if their stomachs are empty. The gnostic Yaḥyā ibn Muʿādh ﵀ once said, revealing the inverse relationship between having wealth and remembering Allah: "Verily, the poor only become happier than the rich because of their remembrance of Allah, for they are in the custody of Allah. If the siege of poverty were to be lifted from them, you would find only a few of them still remembering Allah."[64]

64 Abū Nuʿaym, *Ḥilyah al-Awliyā' wa Ṭabaqāt al-Aṣfiyā'*, vol. 10, p. 62.

Generally, there are two paths to entering Paradise: the Bilāl ibn Rabāḥ ﷺ path and the ʿAbd al-Raḥmān ibn ʿAwf ﷺ path. The first is the path of hardship, while the second is path of generosity. While the majority of people enter Paradise through the Bilāl-trodden path, the Ummah still does need figures following the path of ʿAbd al-Raḥmān ibn ʿAwf ﷺ as well. Nevertheless, the stark reality is that individuals who are materially well-off often fall into gluttony, which causes them to be stripped of their spirituality. Imam al-Muzanī ﷺ said: "You are sufficed in this world with whatever you are content with, even if it is a date, a sip of water, and a bit of shade over your head."[65]

Allah ﷻ has made it abundantly clear that the individuals who become obsessed with the material glitter of others will eventually forget their Creator and fail to pay attention to the wonders that He has promised them. At the superficial level, it may appear that they have everything and have reached the apex, while you are the lowest denominator. But you should never forget that those worn-out articles of clothing that you have in this world will be a form of honour for the believers on the Day of Judgement. The Prophet ﷺ said: "My Ḥawḍ (Fountain)...is whiter than milk and sweeter than honey, and its cups are as numerous as the stars. Whoever drinks from it will never be thirsty again, and the first people to arrive at it will be the poor migrants, with their hair disheveled and their clothes stained, who are not considered for marriage,

65 Ibn Abī Dunyā, *al-Qanāʿah wa al-Taʿaffuf*, p. 62.

and for whom the gates of leaders are not opened."[66] In this report, the Prophet ﷺ is urging his followers to not keep their sights and gazes on the bounties of this world, for they are fleeting and transient. Allah ﷻ is actually replacing your share of sustenance in the next life with rewards, as long as you remain patient. In this regard, Ibn al-Jawzī said: "If you have been prevented from *rizq* in one category, know that you are not prevented from another category."[67] As a result of your material deprivation, Allah ﷻ may have compensated you with another type of benefit or gain, such as righteous friends, loving family members, or a type of rank or honour.

Of course, it is true that in some cases, material deprivation occurs due to one's sins. The Prophet ﷺ said: "Verily the servant is deprived of *rizq* due to a sin he commits." The converse rule is also true, for as Ibn al-Qayyim once said, "Nothing brings *rizq* like leaving off sins." But that type of accrued *rizq* is not necessarily realized in the form of a quantitative gain; occasionally, it might occur in the form of a qualitative improvement in one's lifestyle and mental well-being, for Allah ﷻ may place *barakah* (blessings) in a little bit of gain and destruction in what is perceived to be a relatively high earning.

66 Sunan al-Tirmidhī, 2444.

67 Ibn al-Jawzī, *Ṣayd al-Khāṭir*, p. 190.

From the aforementioned points, the following key dictum can be derived. Allah ﷻ deprives some people due to His love for them in order to raise their rank, but He also does the same to others as a form of punishment in order to lower their rank. Regardless of the reason for this deprivation, a person enjoys the opportunity to benefit from this loss. Either one must recognize their errors and sins and repent to Allah ﷻ or exercise their *riḍā* towards Him to enter. It may be the case that this entire test is a spiritual opportunity for one to exercise their *tawakkul* (reliance) on Allah ﷻ. For as the Prophet said: "If you were to rely upon Allah truly, He would provide for you just as He provides for the birds. They go out in the morning with empty stomachs and they then return full."[68]

By going through these various circumstances, a person is able to appreciate the reality of two of Allah's beautiful attributes, namely al-Bāsiṭ (The One Who Gives) and al-Qābiḍ (The One Who Withholds). If a person goes through pleasant and inflexible material situations, they learn to exercise their trust in Allah ﷻ in both of these states, and their ability to practice Islam becomes stable, regardless of their circumstances. This is why the Prophet ﷺ said:

الطَّاعِمُ الشَّاكِرُ بِمَنْزِلَةِ الصَّائِمِ الصَّابِرِ

"The one who eats and is grateful is just like the one who fasts and is patient."

[68] *Sunan Ibn Mājah*, 4164.

Your spiritual station in this life is guaranteed if you are able to see and recognize Allah ﷻ in times of prosperity and poverty. It is related that on one occasion two Islamic scholars were having a debate, with one of them being materially well-off while the other was poor. The poor one arrived late at the agreed-upon meeting place late and to demonstrate his strategic disadvantage, he apologized and said: "I got distracted because I ran out of oil for my lamp." But the rich scholar responded by saying: "Well, I too was distracted because of how beautiful my chandeliers were." The key takeaway of this story is that both of them were being tested in their own distinctive way, and they were able to recognize Allah through these experiences. Ibn 'Aṭā'allāh al-Iskandarī ﵀ said:

مَتى أَعْطَاكَ أَشْهَدَكَ بِرَّه وَ مَتى مَنَعَكَ أَشْهَدَكَ قَهْرَه
فَهُوَ فِي كُلِّ ذَالِكَ مُتَعَرِّفٌ إِلَيْكَ

"When He gives you, He shows you His Kindness. When He deprives you, He is demonstrating to you His Power. And in all that, He is making Himself known to you and coming closer to you with His Gentleness."

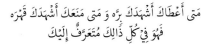

9

Why do I have to carry their burden?

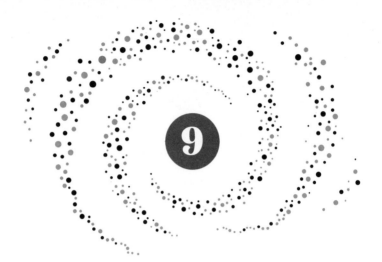

We all have our fair share of burdens in our life, with many factors and objective conditions being beyond our control. This oftentimes leads to frustration and even resentment. A person going through a difficult stage in their day-to-day household life may ask themselves the following questions: "Why do I have to deal with this? I did not choose this family or its problems. I did not even choose to be born!" These types of sentiments usually arise when one feels that an unfair burden is being imposed upon them, such as caring for another family member materially or emotionally in an indefinite manner. Although such trials are undoubtedly challenging, they are means of elevating a person's station and amassing major rewards. Turning away from the Will and Decree of Allah ﷻ can cause a person to lose any moral standing in the sight of their Creator and ruin their prospects in the Hereafter. The attitude and orientation that you take towards a household trial is pivotal in how you will be assessed; if you take it with a smile, that will yield rewards and gifts from your Creator, but if you react with negativity and annoyance, then you risk your salvation in the Hereafter. The Prophet ﷺ is reported to have said: "Whoever relieves a Muslim of a burden from the burdens of this world, Allah will relieve him of a burden from the burdens of the Day of Judgment." Furthermore, the Messenger of Allah ﷺ said: "Whoever helps ease a difficulty in this life, Allah will grant him ease from a difficulty in this life and in the Hereafter." The blessed Prophet ﷺ also said that anyone who covers the faults of a Muslim will have Allah ﷻ cover their faults in this life and the Hereafter.[69]

Humans are short-sighted and lack long-term vision. They often assume that caring for a charge or dependant drains them of their strength and development, being unaware of the fact that they are the source of their present good and survival. This charge or dependant may also be the cause of the expiation of sins done by the caregiver. Instead of closing doors, this supported family member is actually opening them.

69 *Sunan al-Tirmidhī*, 1930.

It is imperative that you view every one of your life's burdens and problems as an opportunity to grow, not a setback or hurdle.

However, on some occasions, one may feel so excessively burdened that they feel that their life is not meaningfully progressing in a linear fashion. But the Muslim must never give up hope, for the Prophet ﷺ expressly said that charity never decreases wealth. In another noteworthy Hadith, he ﷺ said:

مَنْ سَرَّه أَنْ يُبْسَطَ عَلَيْهِ رِزْقه، أَوْيُنْسَأَ لَه فِيْ أَثَرِه، فَلْيَصِلْ رَحْمَه

"Whoever wishes for their sustenance to increase and their years on this Earth to increase should take care of their family ties."[70]

Allah's perfect and complete Decree will never allow a Muslim's beneficent acts to go to waste, since they altruistically spent their time and wealth to serve the interests of a fellow believer, whether in the capacity of a parent or sibling. By doing so, Allah ﷻ will reciprocate by increasing their sustenance and lifespan. What appears to be a burden can actually be a great blessing.

In an astonishing tradition, the Prophet ﷺ mentions an interesting interaction that occurred between two Prophets. He mentioned that Mūsā ﷺ met our forefather Adam ﷺ and said to him:

يَا آدَمُ أَنْتَ أَبُونَا خَيَّبْتَنَا وَأَخْرَجْتَنَا مِنَ الْجَنَّةِ

"O Adam, you are our father, but you let us down and you caused us to be expelled from Paradise due to your sin."

70 *Adab al-Mufrad*, 56.

Adam ﷺ replied to him by saying: "O Mūsā, Allah chose you to speak directly to and He wrote the Tawrāh for you with His own Hand. Are you blaming me for something which Allah decreed for me 40 years before He even created me?" The Prophet ﷺ closed this account by repeating thrice:

فَحَجَّ آدَمُ مُوسَىٰ فَحَجَّ آدَمُ مُوسَىٰ فَحَجَّ آدَمُ مُوسَىٰ

"Thus Adam won the argument against Mūsā."[71]

This does not mean that Islam legitimizes the tenet of original sin, since none of us bear the sin of Adam ﷺ. However it does imply that Islam affirms the original decree, whose effects will endure until the Day of Judgement. In essence, humankind constitutes a perfect continuation of its forefather, since it was destined to live on this Earth, regardless of whether Adam ﷺ committed his wrong or not. While it is true that Adam's deed was the vehicle that caused humanity to be placed in the temporal world, its property as a sin was purely accidental. Without this incident, Mūsā ﷺ—who is own of the greatest Messengers of Allah—would not have been able to lead his heroic battle against Fir'awn (Pharaoh) and liberate the Israelites. Nor would Mūsā ﷺ have been able to meet Khiḍr ﷺ, who repaired the wall of the people who apparently seemed undeserving of this free service.

71 *Ṣaḥīḥ Muslim*, 2652.

But the cause of Khiḍr's benevolent action is explained in the following Quranic verse:

وَكَانَ أَبُوهُمَا صَالِحًا

"And their father had been a righteous man."[72]

This beautiful story requires much reflection, since in it Allah ﷻ rewards these children for acts of righteousness done in the past by their deceased father. The same can be said for us as well; our ancestors and forefathers performed righteous deeds that were decreed to benefit us even before we were born. Someone carried our burden in a past time period and ensured that we would have a relatively easy undertaking, without them being paid or compensated on our part. And just as you may be carrying another person's burden or undertaking in the present moment, Allah ﷻ will send another person to carry yours in the near future. As such, our lives are interconnected; one person's faults brought us in this universe, we are presently forced to tend to others, and in the future other individuals will perform acts on our behalf. The worst thing to do is to deny this reality and to reject the Decree of Allah ﷻ as being unfair or unjust. That is nothing more than the trick of Shayṭān, and as believers, we must avoid such plots lest we be deprived of the Mercy of Allah ﷻ.

---

72 *al-Kahf*, 18:82.

A person should not submit to their base desires in an attempt to abandon their present duties and submit to their selfish desires, thus falling into sin. Allah ﷻ has warned against this pathology in the following verse:

وَلَا تَكُونُوا كَالَّذِينَ نَسُوا اللَّهَ فَأَنسَاهُمْ أَنفُسَهُمْ

"And do not be like those who forgot Allah, so He made them forget themselves."[73]

The one who turns away from Allah ﷻ will damage their own soul and submit to the worst of vices and evil acts. Thus, they will lose their capacity to perform righteous deeds, such as carrying the burdens of their loved ones. Yet even during such dark moments, Allah ﷻ may provide a lost person a lifeline and source of guidance through a sincere friend or family member who helps them re-carry their burden once more. The emergence of such a helper or guide signifies that Allah ﷻ is willing to forgive His lost slave as long as he turns back to his Creator. But if they fail to rectify their ways and repent to Him, they will suffer a life of isolation and suffering.

People who are suffering emotionally are often prone to replicate their conditions to the next generation. As a popular saying goes, "Hurt people hurt people." However, a person does not have to follow such a dark path in their life. For instance, one may consider the example of 'Umar ibn al-Khaṭṭāb رضي الله عنه, who was trapped in a life of trauma due to the abusive conduct of his fathers, even going as far as to succumb to a life of alcoholism.

---

73 *al-Ḥashr,* 59:19.

But after he found the message of Islam and accepted the teachings of the Prophet ﷺ, he said: "O Allah, I am weak, so strengthen me. I am harsh, so make me gentle. I am stingy, so make me generous." He was able to transform every one of his weaknesses into areas of strength and thereby serve Islam to the strongest degree possible.

It is imperative that you view every one of your burdens and problems as an opportunity to grow, not a setback or hurdle. Every perceived difficulty has been decreed by Allah as a means to ensure your smooth transfer to the permanent abode of bliss: Paradise. Ibn 'Aṭā'allāh al-Iskandarī رحمه الله said:

لَا تَرْفَعَنَّ إِلَى غَيْرِهِ حَاجَةً هُوَ مُوْرِدُهَا عَلَيْكَ. فَكَيْفَ يَرْفَعُ غَيْرُهُ مَا
كَانَ هُوَ لَهُ وَاضِعاً مَنْ لَا يَسْتَطِيعُ أَنْ يَرْفَعَ حَاجَةً عَنْ نَفْسِهِ فَكَيْفَ
يَسْتَطِيعُ أَنْ يَكُونَ لَهَا عَنْ غَيْرِهِ رَافِعًا

"Appeal to no one but Him to relieve you of a pressing need that He Himself brought upon you. For how can someone else remove what He has imposed upon you? And how can he who is unable to free himself of a pressing need free anyone else of one?"

10

Did I choose to be Muslim?

Life is full of shocking existential questions which often numb us and cause us to go down the rabbit hole. Such questions intensify even further in cases where we narrowly evade a crisis or pass by a serious wake-up call. Confusion sets in, and we often fail to even grasp any first principles. Perhaps some of the pressing questions that one may ask themselves include the following: "Am I really a believer? What if I just believe because my parents are Muslims? If I do not have faith, what am I?" These spiritual questions are not purposeless or devoid of a benefit. For they cause the Muslim to sincerely search for the meaning of Islam and taste the sweetness of *īmān* (faith).

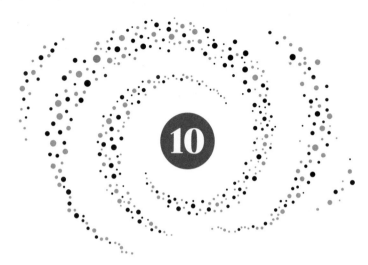

Sometimes through only a shock or surprise can one's faith be strengthened. For the Prophet ﷺ said:

إِنَّ الإِيمَانَ لَيَخْلَقُ فِي جَوْفِ أَحَدِكُمْ كَمَا يَخْلَقُ الثَّوْبُ،
فَاسْأَلُوا اللهَ أَنْ يُجَدِّدَ الإِيمَانَ فِي قُلُوبِكُمْ

"Verily faith wears out in your heart just like a shirt becomes worn out. So ask Allah to renew the faith in your hearts."[74]

A person's *īmān* will fluctuate in accordance with the dictates of the Divine Decree, and as such, it will never be static. There will be certain points in our life where our faith will be of a relatively low level. Shayṭān will attempt to exploit such circumstances and convince the person that having low faith is equivalent to having no faith, such that one could exit the fold of Islam if they wished to do so. But this reasoning is undoubtedly dangerous and incorrect. In actual fact, low faith constitutes a warning sign that one should restore stability in the heart. In some cases, one cannot appreciate the light of faith unless if they are submerged in darkness. In such pivotal moments, Allah ﷻ brings a spark to re-kindle the light of *īmān*.

أَلَمْ يَأْنِ لِلَّذِينَ آمَنُوا أَن تَخْشَعَ قُلُوبُهُمْ لِذِكْرِ اللَّهِ وَمَا نَزَلَ مِنَ الْحَقِّ

"Has the time not yet come for believers' hearts to be humbled at the remembrance of Allah and what has been revealed of the truth?"[75]

---

74 *al-Ṭabarānī, al-Muʿjam al-Kabīr,* 14668. Graded as *ṣaḥīḥ* by al-Albānī.

75 *al-Ḥadīd*, 57:16.

The Muslim knows Who Allah ﷻ is and recognizes the truth, but occasionally needs a firm reminder to become aware of His presence and return to His teachings and dictates. Allah ﷻ will give His slaves a number of chances to attain deliverance, but they must respond with sincerity and urgency. Umar ibn al-Khaṭṭāb ؓ used to say: "I fear a day that Islam will be lost when a generation is born into Islam and does not understand the days of ignorance."

Just for a moment, suppose that you are ʿAbdullāh ibn Khabbāb ibn al-Aratt ؓ. You have the privilege of being born in Medina, which already has an established Muslim community. You enjoy the opportunity to visit the mosque of the Prophet ﷺ on a daily basis, and benefit from his religious instruction as well as that of the senior Companions. But on one occasion, while you are narrating Hadiths from your father Khabbāb ؓ, you notice that he has a number of severe burns on his neck. Such a gruelling sight naturally attracts your attention, and you proceed to ask him why they are there. He then relates to you his life experiences in Mecca, where he was enslaved and how his master would pour hot coal down his back and other parts of his body because he believed in the message of Islam. Compared to his father, ʿAbdullāh's life was one of privilege and deep comforts, but without the sacrifices of the father, his son would have never seen such bounties. In light of all the pains and struggles he had to go through, Khabbāb ؓ immensely treasured his faith. These stories should inspire us to rekindle our faith in any feasible manner.

Oftentimes, our lack of faith stems from one of two things: 1) an intellectual quandary concerning a particular issue or tenet in Islam, or 2) unresolved mental trauma. In the first case, the solution is to ask a trained and trusted specialist of the faith with an open heart. The Prophet ﷺ is reported to have said: "The cure of ignorance is just to ask a question." If one is sincere, they will be able to find convincing answers that will extinguish the doubts of any reasonable person. Even in cases where an answer may not fully agree with your sensibilities, you should submit to the fact that Allah ﷻ indeed always knows best, His revelation is perfect, and that the Prophet ﷺ is truly His Messenger.

Unfortunately, however, it is often the case that we misdiagnose a bad life experience as a genuine intellectual problem. For example, one may have a female family member who was abused by her husband and then use this experience as a pretext to blame Islam for his behaviours. While such feelings may be somewhat understandable, they still cannot be justified. For example, when the Prophet Mūsā ﷺ saw al-Khiḍr ﷺ kill a young boy, he was horrified by this sight, especially because it reminded him of the genocidal campaign that Firʿawn led against the children of the Israelites, which he was saved from due to the divine facilitation of Allah ﷻ. Yet, even while criticizing al-Khiḍr ﷺ for this apparent wrong, he did not utter anything against his Creator or the religion that he belonged to; he simply sought an answer or rationale for this action. This should be the course of action undertaken by the believer, whereby they have perfect faith and reliance on the Wisdom of their Lord, Who is al-Khabīr (The Perfectly-Informed One). Quite paradoxically, sins can potentially be used as a means to elevate one's station. Just like how uttering the *shahādah* (proclamation of faith) erases a person's past sins and wrongs, sincere *tawbah* (repentance) provides a person a clean slate. When the noble Companion Ka'b ibn Mālik ﷺ repented for failing to attend the expedition of Tabūk, Allah ﷻ showered him with His Mercy and raised his rank to an unforeseen level. The Prophet congratulated him by saying:

أَبْشِرْ بِخَيْرِ يَومٍ مَرَّ عَلَيْكَ مُنْذُ وَلَدَتْكَ أُمُّك

"Receive glad tidings of the best day of your life since your mother gave birth to you."

Whether it is the first time someone enters Islam or an episode of repentance, turning to Allah constitutes a rebirth and re-awakening. In the case of Ka'b ibn Mālik ﷺ, it was a sin that sparked his ability to turn back to his Creator. Every Muslim can learn from this historical episode, and try to reflect on their past lapses and sins and use them as a catalyst to spark their redemption. Should they do this, then they will have their sins converted into good deeds.

In this regard, Allah ﷻ states:

فَأُولَئِكَ يُبَدِّلُ اللَّهُ سَيِّئَاتِهِمْ حَسَنَاتٍ وَكَانَ اللَّهُ غَفُورًا رَحِيمًا

"They are the ones whose evil deeds Allah will change into good deeds."[76]

76 *al-Furqān*, 25:70.

The Muslim knows Who Allah ﷻ is and recognizes the truth, but occasionally needs a firm reminder to become aware of His presence and return to His teachings and dictates.

As Ibn al-Qayyim once poignantly said, a sin that brings a person back to Allah is superior to a good deeds that causes one to become distant from him. From this viewpoint, a sin can actually be a good dynamic as it gives one the drive and humility to return back to Allah. Sometimes, a spark like this is needed, such as reflecting on the consequences of one's sins or how the lack of any spirituality and remembrance of Allah creates a void in one's life, even if one is successful at the material level in this world. Every person who was born in the wrong faith and converted to Islam is acutely aware of this reality, and recognizes the unlimited sweetness in the message of the true religion of Allah. Every sacrifice they had to make in order to facilitate their conversion will be handsomely rewarded by Allah. As for the person who was born and raised as a Muslim, then they should appreciate that Allah decreed that they be born on the path of guidance, which in essence allowed them to enjoy an early start in their spiritual journey. They should capitalize on this divine facilitation and ensure that they do not squander their spiritual advantage by praying: "O Allah, You granted me Islam and I did not even ask you for it. So grant me Paradise, and I am asking you for it." Our lives will be filled with events which will cause us to ponder over why we are Muslims in the first place and how much we wish to abide by our religion's dictates. Ensure that you always purify and renew your intention and strive to orient yourself in a way that pleases your Lord.

Ibn ʿAṭāʾallāh al-Iskandarī ﵀ said in one of his aphorisms:

لا يُخَافُ عَلَيْكَ أَنْ تَلْتَبِسَ الطُّرِيْقُ عَلَيْكَ؛ وَإِنَّمَا يُخَافُ عَلَيْكَ مِنْ غَلَبَةِ الهَوَى عَلَيْكَ

"What is feared is not that the ways leading to Allah will be confusing to you. Rather what is feared is that your desires will overcome you."

Say, "Nothing will ever befall us except what Allah has destined for us. He is our Protector." So in Allah let the believers put their trust.

AL-TAUBAH, 51

11

Why is Allah not answering me?

During times of difficulty and tribulation, we are often told to turn back to Allah ﷻ and pray to Him earnestly. But sometimes it may appear to us that our desperate pleas and calls to Allah ﷻ are not being answered or addressed. This naturally leads to the question of whether our *duʿāʾ* (supplication) is being heard and if we will ever receive an answer. There is a relevant report from the noble Companion Salmān al-Fārisī ؓ which addresses this perplexing problem. In it, Salmān ؓ states:

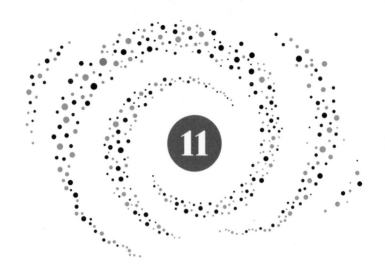

إِذَا كَانَ الرَّجُلُ دَعَّاءً فِي السَّرَّاءِ ثُمَّ نَزَلَتْ بِهِ ضَرَّاءُ فَدَعَا قَالَتِ الْمَلَائِكَةُ : صَوْتٌ مَعْرُوفٌ اسْتَغْفِرُوا لَهُ ، وَإِذَا كَانَ الرَّجُلُ لَيْسَ بِدَعَّاءٍ فِي السَّرَّاءِ فَنَزَلَتْ بِهِ ضَرَّاءُ فَدَعَا قَالَتِ الْمَلَائِكَةُ : صَوْتٌ لَيْسَ بِمَعْرُوفٍ وَلَا يَشْفَعُونَ لَهُ

"If a man who is accustomed to making du'ā' in good times goes through a hardship and then makes a du'ā', his voice travels through the heavens. The Angels say among themselves: 'That is a familiar voice; let us go and intercede with Allah on his behalf.' But if a person is not accustomed to making du'ā' in good times and a hardship comes upon him, then should he make du'ā' to Allah the Angels will say to themselves: 'That is not a voice that we usually hear.' As such, they do not bother to intercede on his behalf."

A moment of genuine introspection is needed, where one asks themselves: "How often does my voice travel through the heavens?" Is it only when everything in one's life is going apart? The key moral lesson that one should derive from the themes of making *du'ā'* to Allah ﷻ and hardship is that establishing a relationship with Allah ﷻ should never be predicated on the concept of hardship in the first place. When the Prophet Ibrāhīm ﷺ turned to Allah in his most difficult moment, he addressed Him as a close guardian and helper that he was already well-familiar with:

إِنَّ رَبِّي لَسَمِيعُ الدُّعَاءِ

"My Lord is indeed the Hearer of prayers."[77]

77 *Ibrāhīm*, 14:39.

In a similar fashion, when the noble Prophet Zakariyyā ﵇ called to Allah ﷻ in his supplication, he made a clear indication that he would often pray and seek the succour of his Lord:

وَلَمْ أَكُنْ بِدُعَآئِكَ رَبِّ شَقِيًّا

"I have never been disappointed in my prayer to You, my Lord!"[78]

Zakariyyā's gratefulness to his Lord is astonishing. By no means was he a wealthy person. Instead, he lived a very humble life as a carpenter and remained fatherless until his 90s. Yet, here in his prayer he is thanking Allah ﷻ for always providing him assistance. This should be the mentality of the believer.

How do these moral lessons apply to one in the contemporary setting? You may have prayed to Allah ﷻ with sincerity and exerted your soundest efforts to lead a moral ethical life. Despite these efforts, you eventually succumb to the temptation of sin and revert back to your old deadly habits. Despite reaching out to Allah ﷻ on a regular basis, you actually now feel more distant from Him. In the face of such hardships, how can one feel optimistic and maintain a positive relationship with Allah ﷻ?

---

78 *Maryam*, 19:4.

The Prophet ﷺ provided a succinct response to this quandary when he said:

الدُّعَاءُ هُوَ الْعِبَادَةُ

"Du'ā' is [the essence of] worship."

In light of this report, one cannot simply worship during pressing and difficult circumstances. The Prophet ﷺ would regularly supplicate to Allah ﷻ in his prayers, and would often make lengthy *du'ā's* in his *sujūd* (prostration), such that he would weep. Anybody who witnessed the Prophet ﷺ in this state would assume that a tragedy or hurtful event had occurred, but the reality was that it constituted a regular portion of the Prophet's routine. Whether he was in a time of hardship or ease, he turned to his Creator.

For the general masses of the Muslim Ummah, however, hardship is sometimes ordained by Allah ﷻ in order to awaken His heedless servants and cause them to reflect on the underpinnings of their worldly existence. Just as a sin can cause a person to turn to Allah ﷻ in repentance, worldly hardships can be the driver that allows them to fall in love with Him. If one sincerely calls upon Allah ﷻ on a regular basis, they will begin to attain closer proximity to Him and become attentive of His presence, even if the hardship in question has not been removed yet.

Turn to Him with confidence, and you will eventually receive a positive response. The Prophet ﷺ said:

اُدْعُوا اللَّهَ وَأَنْتُمْ مُوقِنُونَ بِالْإِجَابَةِ

"Call upon Allah while you are certain in the answer."

And Allah ﷻ Himself said in His Book:

وَإِذَا سَأَلَكَ عِبَادِي عَنِّي فَإِنِّي قَرِيبٌ ۖ أُجِيبُ دَعْوَةَ الدَّاعِ إِذَا دَعَانِ

"When My servants ask you about Me:
I am truly near. I respond to one's prayer
when they call upon Me."[79]

The believer should always internalize these proof-texts and have full trust in their Lord's Wisdom. The pious folk and friends of Allah ﷻ were never worried if a divine response was not received immediately. This is why ʿUmar ibn al-Khaṭṭāb رضي الله عنه said that he never felt perplexed with regard to receiving a positive answer for his *duʿā'*, since he had no doubt that Allah ﷻ would please His slave with good. In other words, once a believer sincerely supplicates to their Lord, they have already attained the greatest outcome, which is being able to have a conversation with Him. And if they wait patiently for a response, they will attain an even greater reward.

---

[79] *al-Baqarah,* 2:186.

In this regard, the Prophet ﷺ said:

سَلُوا اللَّهَ مِنْ فَضْلِهِ فَإِنَّ اللَّهَ يُحِبُّ أَنْ يُسْأَلَ وَأَفْضَلُ الْعِبَادَةِ انْتِظَارُ الْفَرَجِ

"Ask Allah for His bounties, as Allah loves to be asked. And amongst the best acts of worship is to patiently wait and have the expectation of relief."[80]

But the Prophet ﷺ warned people from becoming dissatisfied if they do not receive a response. He said: "Allah will answer [His slave] until they say, 'I prayed continuously and He did not answer me." Such a mentality can potentially destroy any goodness that would have been allotted had patience been observed. In this regard, the Prophet said: "Nothing repels the Divine Decree but supplication, and nothing increases a person's lifespan except for good deeds."[81]

The Prophet ﷺ said that a sincere *du'ā'* repels bad deeds and good deeds maximize a person's good decree. But in this context, what exactly do the terms good and bad entail? Perhaps one of the most fascinating aspects pertaining to *du'ā'* is that Allah gives His servant what is best for them, which may not necessarily correspond to what they seek or desire. In other words, Allah ﷻ does not answer His servant in the way that his servant wants to be answered, but in the way that he needs to be answered. In an important Hadith, the Prophet ﷺ said that Allah ﷻ responds to a *du'ā'* in one of

80 *Sunan al-Tirmidhī*, 3571.

81 *Sunan al-Tirmidhī*, 2139.

three ways: 1) responding to the supplication immediately, 2) store its good for His servant in the Hereafter, or 3) remove an equivalent evil to it.[82] For instance, Allah ﷻ can respond to a person's *du'ā'* for passing an exam by reversing a calamity that would have claimed the life of a relative. He may not respond to a person's plea for a career in one field since He has decreed for them a job in an even superior area, or, he may not wish to positively respond to a person's request in this world since He has stored for them unimaginable rewards in the Hereafter.

A person cannot sincerely supplicate to Allah ﷻ for a desired outcome unless they forego the sins and bad habits that impede the passage of our prayers to their Creator. The great Muslim ascetic Ibrāhīm ibn Adham رحمه الله was once asked why many of our *du'ā's* to Allah ﷻ remain unanswered. Ibrāhīm ibn Adham رحمه الله responded by saying: "It is because you know Allah and you do not obey Him. You know the Messenger ﷺ and you do not follow him. You know the Qur'an and you do not act according to it. You eat from the blessings of Allah and you do not thank Him. You eat from the blessings of Allah and you do not thank Him for it. You know Paradise and you do not seek it. You know the Hellfire and you do not flee from it. You know the Shayṭān and you do not fight him; instead, you follow him. You know death and you do not prepare for it. You bury the dead and you do not learn from it. You ignore

82 *Musnad Imām Aḥmad*, 11133.

your faults, and you busy yourself with the faults of others."[83] Echoing this grand sentiment, Ibn 'Aṭā'allāh al-Iskandarī رحمه الله also said:

لا تُطَالِبْ رَبَّكَ بِتَأَخُّرِ مَطْلَبِكَ وَلٰكِنْ طَالِبْ نَفْسَكَ بِتَأَخُّرِ أَدَبِك

"Do not press claims against your Lord because your request has been delayed. Instead, press claims against yourself for lacking in your behaviour."

Strive to remove the barriers that presently exist between yourself and your Creator, and then you will be able to capitalize on the blessings and provisions that are embedded in *du'ā'*. If you do not change your lifestyle habits and lead an ethical life that is informed by the teachings of the religion, then you will never be able to taste the sweetness and divine facilitation that comes with *du'ā'*. Your progress will always be stunted. Call upon your Lord with confidence, patience, and mental resolve, and over time you will see your life be transformed and elevated to an unforeseen degree.

83 *Tafsīr al-Qurṭubī for Qur'an*, 2:186.

12

Why make *Istikhārah?*

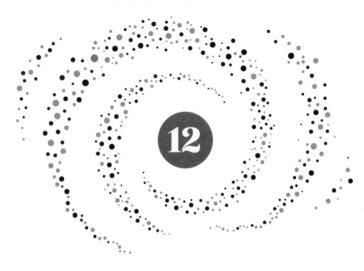

You are now regularly addressing Allah ﷻ, enjoying your spiritual proximity to Him, and making *du'ā'* to Him consistently and confidently. But life is full of unusual twists and turns, and sometimes you have to successfully traverse major milestones in life, such as decisions pertaining to one's career, spouse, country of residence, and so on. Such major events create a high degree of stress in a person's mind, as they are often forced to choose between a number of available options, with no clear tiebreaker between them. Fortunately, Allah ﷻ has provided us a number of measures to solve such problems, such as the principle of *istishārah* (consultation) and a special prayer known as *ṣalāh al-istikhārah*. Regarding the two, Imam al-Nawawī said: "No person ever regrets *istishārah* and *istikhārah*." By capitalizing on these various prayers, a person will have done their best to seek positive results, and must then await the response of their Lord.

The positive result that one expects may not materialize in an express fashion; instead, one must go through a detour in order to traverse a learning experience. For instance, in this regard one may consider the story of the Prophet ﷺ in Mecca. For 13 years, the Prophet ﷺ had prayed to Allah ﷻ for the guidance of his people, while the nascent Muslim community faced immense persecution at the hands of the polytheist community. Despite the immense hardships and torture that both he and his followers experienced, he continued to make *du'ā'* to Allah ﷻ, with some of his prayers being equivalent to the intensity and vigour found in *istikhārah*. The Prophet ﷺ was of the hope that these prayers would allow him to receive safe refuge in the city of Ṭā'if. But these hopes almost instantly evaporated, as the inhabitants of the city harshly abused the Prophet ﷺ and expelled him. Not only was the Prophet ﷺ now rejected in Mecca, but he was also given an unwelcome reception in Ṭā'if as well.

In our own life stories, we may see similar parallels to this past historical episode. We may pray earnestly to Allah ﷻ for a job or marriage, but after we are granted them, we end up suffering and finding out that they were completely different from what was originally envisioned. But this initial stage of failure can be a springboard for a greater and more enduring form of success. In this regard, one may look at the story of the Prophet Zakariyyā ﷺ. For numerous decades, he prayed to Allah for a child, but he and his wife remained without any children. They had to be extremely patient in order to receive a positive response from the Divine. But this delay had its inherent wisdom: for their patience and persistent *du'ā's*, Allah ﷻ stored for their other-worldly accounts an endless store of rewards. Likewise, this delay had another benefit: because he did not have to tend to any of his own children, Zakariyyā ﷺ had the time and resources to take care of Maryam, and ensure that her needs were met as she studied the religion of Allah ﷻ. Thus, Allah's delay in positively responding to Zakariyyā's prayer was replete with benefits. The same can be said with regard to the blessed Prophet ﷺ; although he was unable to win the hearts of the people of Mecca and Ṭā'if, he was eventually granted an even greater homeland in Medina.

The *istikhārah* prayer contains a special supplication where one feels lost at a particular intersection of life, and asks Allah ﷻ to grant them what is best for them in this world and the Hereafter. Issues arise whenever we feel that our prayers are not causing us to attain any tangible progress, and we are stuck at a particular point. A desired marriage may not occur or fail to materialize in the intended fashion, or a highly-pursued career may slip by. At such a point, many people become tempted to ask, "What was the point of my *du'ā'*?"

The wise believer must know that the prayer of *istikhārah* entails asking for two things: goodness in this world and the Hereafter. For some individuals and personalities, these two aims may be in conflict, or it may be the case that a particular result is needed owing to one's point at their spiritual journey. Allah ﷻ may have decreed to only grant His servant his particular desire or want only after they achieve an elevation in their spiritual rank and character.

If a person could witness the full Wisdom of Allah ﷻ and the long-term plan that He has destined for them, they would not only be understanding, but also grateful. Ibn Qayyim al-Jawziyyah ﷺ once said: "If the veils were lifted and you could see behind the scenes what Allah does out of kindness for you, your heart would melt out of love for Him."[84] In his opinion, the main problem is that many Muslims have a deformed state of *tawakkul* (reliance), in which they not only wish for a particular end in life but, also demand a specific route and pathway to it as well. Such a person is short-sighted and unaware of the mysteries of fate; they do not realize that could have experienced a different version of life and undergone an entirely different trajectory.

Every day when you go outside in the external world, you are likely coming across different versions of yourself, that is, people who are strikingly similar to you but trekking divergent paths. It may be that in your view, some of those

---

[84] Ibn al-Qayyim, *Ṭarīq al-Hijratayn*, p. 180.

individuals are leading better lives than you. You could have been in the place of one of them, but there is no guarantee that you would be in a better spiritual rank. The sole factor that should concern the believer is the following: any life state that causes a person to return back to Allah ﷻ is the best for them, regardless of the time or context. For this reason, Sufyān ibn 'Uyaynah ؒ said: "What the servant hates is better for him than what he loves, because what he hates will cause him to increase in his *du'ā'*, and what he loves will distract him from *du'ā'*."

The more the response to your prayers are delayed, the more desperate and genuine your pleas to your Creator will become. Your eyes will become tearful and you will begin to call upon Allah ﷻ with His majestic and honourable names, some of which you did not use before. As such, your connection with Allah ﷻ will become more insensitive and intimate. This will ultimately bring forth the ultimate realization that the delay of the divine response was actually the greatest gift imaginable.

And as time passes and the need becomes more urgent, your prayers become more urgent as well. The more those tears start to flow from your eyes, the more you start to call out to Allah ﷻ by names you didn't even know before. You will connect with Allah on a higher level than ever.

Then you will realize that the delay along the way was actually the greatest gift. In his famous book on aphorisms, Ibn ʿAṭāʾallāh al-Iskandarī رحمه الله said:

لَا يَكُنْ تَأَخُّرُ أَمَدِ العَطَاءِ مَعَ الإِلْحَاحِ فِي الدُّعَاءِ مُوْجِباً لِيَأْسِكَ. فَهُوَ ضَمِنَ لَكَ الإِجَابَةَ
فِيمَا يَخْتَارُهُ لَكَ لَا فِيمَا تَخْتَارُهُ لِنَفْسِكَ. وَفِي الوَقْتِ الَّذِي يُرِيدُ لَا فِي الوَقْتِ الَّذِي تُرِيدُ

"If in spite of intense supplication, there is a delay in the timing of the gift, let that not be the cause for your despair. For He has guaranteed you a response in what He chooses for you, not in what you choose for yourself, and at the time He wills, not the time you desire."

The recipe of success is becoming non-insistent and non-committal to the requested outcome. One can and should pray to Allah ﷻ, but they should maintain a tranquil demeanour even if they are not receiving a response. Submit to Allah ﷻ with full humility, trust His judgement, and Allah ﷻ will recompense you in the best way possible.

13

Will I ever find true love?

Does the concept of love at first sight exist in Islam? Is there really such a thing as true love? Does Islam accept the notion of soulmates? These questions are quite naturally and intuitively posed by many Muslims, who wonder whether their marital relationships have been set in the Divine Decree. The answers for these questions can be found in the generality of the Islamic evidences, which all provide an affirmative answer.

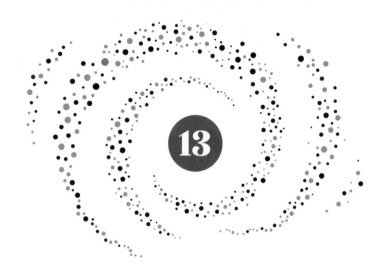

The first relevant proof-text for this question is a beautiful Hadith of the Prophet ﷺ that states:

الْأَرْوَاحُ جُنُودٌ مُجَنَّدَةٌ

"Souls are like conscripted soldiers."

The background event which caused the Prophet ﷺ to utter this statement is quite fascinating. In this regard, 'Ā'ishah ﵂ relates that in Mecca there was a woman who had an incredible sense of humour, such that her amusing tales would cause everyone present at a given gathering to laugh. It so happened that after undertaking the Hijrah to Medina, another woman in the latter city possessed the same humorous touch as the Meccan woman. This like-mindedness surprised 'Ā'ishah ﵂ so much that she shared this observation with the Prophet ﷺ, which caused him to say: "Souls are like conscripted soldiers. They incline towards one another based upon this natural affinity."[85]

There are strong indicators that a romantic analogue of this affinity exists as well. It is related that once a Muslim scholar said to his wife: "Is it not amazing that 50,000 years prior Allah ﷻ brought into existence the heavens and the Earth? He put your name next to mine."

---

85 *Ṣaḥīḥ Muslim*, 2638.

The Prophet ﷺ urged individuals wishing to get married to prioritize the factors of religion and character. Unlike physical beauty, which fades away with time, these elements constitute intangible forms of beauty that will allow a couple to thrive for eternity.

With this statement, he was alluding to the following Quranic verse:

وَمِنْ ءَايَٰتِهِۦٓ أَنْ خَلَقَ لَكُم مِّنْ أَنفُسِكُمْ أَزْوَٰجًا لِّتَسْكُنُوٓا۟ إِلَيْهَا وَجَعَلَ بَيْنَكُم مَّوَدَّةً وَرَحْمَةً إِنَّ فِى ذَٰلِكَ لَءَايَٰتٍ لِّقَوْمٍ يَتَفَكَّرُونَ

"And one of His signs is that He created for you spouses from among yourselves so that you may find comfort in them. And He has placed between you compassion and mercy. Surely in this are signs for people who reflect."[86]

This type of affinity can be observed when a person meets a person that they fall in love with, whereby they can innately perceive that this is the person that they will live with for the rest of their life. Once this baseline level of attraction is found, love can settle in the heart quite rapidly in an unanticipated manner. This is why Imam Ibn Ḥazm ﵀ once said:

أَلْحُبُّ أَوَّلُه هَزْلٌ وَ آخِرُه جَدّ

"Love starts off as something very playful, and then it proceeds to something very serious."[87]

In fact, the Imam ﵀ also mentions that the meanings embedded in love are so profound that they are not amenable to description. Instead, the whole experience of falling in love with someone is so profound that it can only be understood through experience. Furthermore, this great Imam states

86 *al-Rūm*, 30:21.

87 Ibn Ḥazm, *Ṭawq al-Ḥamāmah*, p. 5.

that love is not actually a blameworthy concept in the Islamic ethos nor is it deemed forbidden, since every heart is under the control of Allah ﷻ.

Because it is not fully under the control of a person, love—especially falling in love—is a divine test. In other words, it is something that Allah ﷻ decrees in a person's heart. As long as a person does not pursue and act upon this love in a wrongful manner and abides by the dictates of the Shariah, then they will not be blameworthy in any sense. In fact, they can accrue rewards if they pursue this love and affection through the Islamic institution of marriage. This latter point is reflected in the following verse:

إِنَّ فِي ذَٰلِكَ لَآيَٰتٍ لِّقَوْمٍ يَتَفَكَّرُونَ

"Surely in this are signs for people who reflect."[88]

Some exegetes and commentators have noted that the signs alluded to in this verse are the special names of Allah ﷻ whose effects are most strongly realized in the relations between the two spouses. For instance, within the institution of marriage, one most strongly observes the power of Allah's name *al-Wadūd* (The Most Loving), and the unique manifestations of His compassion in His name *al-Raḥmān* (The Most Merciful).

---

88 *al-Rūm*, 30:21.

The blessed *sīrah* (biography) of the Prophet ﷺ reveals a number of love stories, with some being beautiful, others being sad and tragic, and a third category consisting of grey borderline cases. Cases of the first include the unions that the Prophet ﷺ had with his various wives, as well as the marriage between ʿAlī ibn Abī Ṭālib and Fāṭimah ‹. As for the third case, there is the famous story of Muhājir Umm Qays ‹, who was a man that made Hijrah from Mecca to Medina. This trip was not made to seek Allah's pleasure or to escape from the persecution meted by the polytheists, but simply in order to marry a woman by the name of Umm Qays ‹. As such, he became known as Muhājir Umm Qays, namely the man who travelled for Umm Qays. The Prophet ﷺ did not condemn this man for undertaking such a course of action, but he did allude to the fact that such a person cannot claim the reward of the Hijrah if their intent was solely to marry.[89]

A heartbreaking and tragic story is that of Barīrah and Mughīth ‹, both of whom were slaves that were married during their period of bondage. But after ʿĀ'ishah ‹ had her emancipated, Barīrah ‹ opted to separate from her husband Mughīth ‹. Mughīth's heart was broken with this decision, and he would chase after Barīrah ‹, begging her to reconsider. This scene caused many of the inhabitants of Medina to feel sorry for Mughīth ‹, as he was sobbing uncontrollably. But Barīrah ‹ did not feel any attraction towards Mughīth, which eliminated the possibility of reconciliation between them.

---

[89] *Ṣaḥīḥ al-Bukhārī*, 1.

The Prophet ﷺ was amazed by this sight, such that he exclaimed: "Is it not astonishing how much Mughīth loves her and how much Barīrah hates him?" The Prophet ﷺ attempted to re-unite them and suggested to Barīrah ﷺ, "Will you not take him back?" Barīrah ﷺ said: "O Messenger of Allah, are you commanding me to do so or are you simply interceding?" The Prophet ﷺ said: "No, I am just interceding." In response to this, Barīrah ﷺ said: "I have no need for him, O Messenger of Allah."The Prophet ﷺ then let the matter go, which was a subtle indication to Mughīth ﷺ that Allah's Decree did not destine them to be together; the solution for him was to move on. While it is true that love is based on one's personal desire, it is primarily dictated by the Divine Decree set by the Creator. In other words, a person's love story is written by Allah ﷻ in the heavens before one is even born in this world.

In his work on love theory, Imam Ibn Ḥazm ﷺ enumerates more than 15 reasons for why people fall in love. Some of the key features which he outlines include physical beauty, character, a sound and balanced temperament, nobility, good character, wealth, lineage, and other distinctive features. But the Imam states that the most noble form of love is the category known as *maḥabbah al-mutaḥābayn fī Allāh*, which refers to when two people love each other for the sake of Allah ﷻ. Such a mutual form of love could exist due to the two parties sharing a similar passion and internal drive for performing righteous deeds. When such a strong affinity exists, marriage should be pursued, since it will make this love permissible. The Prophet ﷺ said:

لَمْ نَرَ لِلْمُتَحَابَّيْنِ مِثْلَ النِّكَاحِ

*"We know of nothing better for two people who
love each other than to get married."*

The Prophet ﷺ urged individuals wishing to get married
to prioritize the factors of religion and character. Unlike
physical beauty, which fades away with the passage of time,
these aforementioned elements constitute intangible forms
of beauty that will allow a couple to thrive for eternity. Of
course, this does not mean that other factors are unimportant
or non-foundational. It is related that the Companion al-
Mughīrah ibn Shuʿbah ؓ was interested in marrying with an
individual, and the Prophet ﷺ asked him:

هَلْ نَظَرْتَ إِلَيْهَا؟

"Did you go look at her?"

Al-Mughīrah ؓ replied in the negative. The Prophet ﷺ
subsequently said:

أُنْظُرْ إِلَيْهَا فَإِنَّهُ أَحْرَى أَنْ يُؤْدَمَ بَيْنَكُمَا

*"Then go look at her, because it is better that
there should be love between you."*

Even when all these positive factors and conditions are met,
it might be Allah's Decree that the marriage between two
compatible individuals break down and they consequently
separate. While this reality may be uncomfortable for many

individuals, it is the nature of this world, such that even the most "perfect" and "ideal" union can be destined to fail. The true and sincere believer submits to this fact and is content with this decree. Even if they do not find their soulmate in this world, they know that Allah ﷻ has promised them a beautiful partner in the gardens of Paradise. This is the guarantee of the Creator to the believing members of His creation. The Prophet ﷺ said:

لَيْسَ فِي الْجَنَّةِ أَعْزَب

"There will be no single people in Paradise."

Some of the best and closest friends of Allah ﷻ had non-existent or repugnant spouses. In the latter category, one may consider the case of Āsiyah, who was one of the best women to walk on this Earth, although her husband was an arrogant disbeliever and tyrant who refused to submit to the orders of Allah ﷻ. As for the first category, one may list Maryam, who was the greatest woman of her time and the mother of a Prophet. Despite her hefty list of virtues, Maryam never married in her life. Within the Muslim Ummah, there were a number of notable scholars who opted to forego marriage so they would be able to spend all their time and resources to serve the religion of Allah. The names of these figures are enumerated in a beautiful work penned by the late Hadith scholar Shaykh ʿAbd al-Fattāḥ Abū Ghuddah ﵀, which is entitled as *al-ʿUlamāʾ al-ʿUzzāb aladhīna Ātharū al-ʿIlm ʿalā al-Zawāj* (*The Unmarried Scholars Who Preferred Knowledge Over Marriage*). Some of the notable figures that are mentioned in this book include Imams al-Ṭabarī, al-Nawawī, Ibn Taymiyyah, and the famous ascetic Rābiʿah al-ʿAdawiyyah ﷺ. While these luminous figures did not have any children or direct descendants, they were able to leave behind something far more precious: sacred knowledge. Every one of them garnered a circle of faithful students who preserved their words and ensured that it would benefit countless generations in the future. Thus, although these scholars were deprived of the opportunity to marry, they received a priceless form of *rizq* (provision) that will register for them countless rewards in the Hereafter.

If a person is currently struggling to find a righteous spouse, they should never despair of the Mercy of Allah ﷻ and His provisions; their soulmate may be both temporally and physically near to them, such that they will cross paths with them in the proximate future. It is reported that the noble Companion Abū Hurayrah ﷺ was unable to get married due to his poverty, and as such, he approached the Prophet ﷺ and complained of his state. The Prophet ﷺ listened to his complaints and then repeated thrice:

جَفَّ الْقَلَمُ بِمَا أَنْتَ لاَقٍ

"The pen has dried with what you are going to find."[90]

In other words, the Prophet ﷺ was stressing to Abū Hurayrah ﷺ that he will inevitably receive what has been mentioned in his name. And just as he promised, it so happened that several years

[90] *Ṣaḥīḥ al-Bukhārī,* 5072.

later Abū Hurayrah ؓ was able to marry. Every person should be optimistic that their Lord has prepared for them what is best for them in this life and the next. But patience is always a required element. There are some narrations which state that after he descends and returns to the Earth, Prophet ʿĪsā ؑ will finally marry. This means that he will have to wait thousands of years to meet his soulmate. This account should serve as a reminder that the righteous and friends of Allah should always be optimistic and be hopeful of their Lord's Grace. On this pertinent matter, Ibn ʿAṭā'allāh al-Iskandarī ؒ said:

مَنْ ظَنَّ انْفِكاكَ لُطْفِهِ عَنْ قَدَرِهِ فَذلِكَ لِقُصورِ نَظَرِه

"Whoever supposes that His loving Kindness is separate from His ordaining Decree does so out of his own short-sightedness."

Thus, place your trust in Allah ﷻ and submit to His Will, for he has stored for you what is best and will recompense you handsomely if you maintain a positive disposition and lead a life that revolves around His remembrance.

If a person is currently struggling to find a righteous spouse, they should never despair of the Mercy of Allah ﷻ and His provisions; their soulmate may be both temporally and physically near to them, such that they will cross paths with them in the proximate future.

14

Why were hurtful people put in my life?

Throughout the course of our respective lifetimes, we will cross paths with people who will break our hearts and fill our minds with sadness. We may face betrayal and indignation from our close loved ones and family members, which naturally will cause one to ask why Allah ﷻ placed such people in our paths and why we have to face mental and spiritual damage from individuals who apparently share so many common features with us. A preliminary answer to this pressing query can be found in the following Quranic verse:

خُذِ ٱلْعَفْوَ وَأْمُرْ بِٱلْعُرْفِ وَأَعْرِضْ عَنِ ٱلْجَٰهِلِينَ

***"Be gracious, enjoin what is right, and turn away from those who act ignorantly."*[91]**

After this verse was revealed, the Prophet ﷺ asked Jibrīl ﷺ to clarify what this imperative meant. In response, Jibrīl ﷺ said: "I will not know until I ask my Lord." After receiving a direct response from Allah ﷻ, Jibrīl ﷺ returned to the Prophet ﷺ and said: "Verily, Allah commands you to reconcile with those who cut you off, to give to those who deprive you, and to pardon those who wrong you."[92] The Prophet ﷺ lived by this imperative throughout his life. In fact, after the Prophet ﷺ passed away, his sword was given to his cousin and son-in-law ʿAlī ﷺ. After perusing the sword, ʿAlī ﷺ noticed that the following words were engraved on it:

أُعْفُ عَنْ مَنْ ظَلَمَكَ وَ صِلْ مَنْ قَطَعَكَ وَأَحْسِنْ إِلَى
مَنْ أَسَاءَ إِلَيْكَ وَقُلِ الْحَقَّ وَلَوْ عَلَى نَفْسِكَ

"Forgive those who have wronged you, reconcile with those who have cut you off, show excellence to those who have shown you evil, and speak the truth even if it is against yourself."

---

91 *al-Aʿrāf*, 7:199.

92 *Tafsīr al-Ṭabarī for Qur'an*, 7:199.

Notwithstanding His grandeur, power, and majesty, Allah ﷻ inscribed the following words on His Throne: "My mercy overcomes My anger." Moreover, He sent His final Prophet ﷺ to the entire creation as a mercy of the worlds. This edict was upheld to the extent that the Prophet ﷺ inscribed his own sword—an object used for war and fighting—with a motto of mercy. From these aforementioned points, one internalizes a pertinent prophetic reality, which is that one must have the fortitude to curb one's answer and treat all people with grace, even those who imposed a wrong or injustice upon them. The spirit of forgiveness is perhaps most clearly exemplified in the story of Prophet Yūsuf عليه السلام, who pardoned his brothers for their wrongful conduct towards him, and the Messenger of Allah ﷺ, who exonerated the people of Quraysh for their persecution and torture of the Muslims. They were the best of people who were forced to endure harms meted by the worst of people, yet they persevered with smiles on their faces. This golden standard was emulated by the great Companion Abū Bakr al-Ṣiddīq رضي الله عنه, who forgave a man by the name of Misṭaḥ ibn Athathah رضي الله عنه who partook in the vicious slander against his pure daughter. At first, Abū Bakr رضي الله عنه swore that he would no longer provide Misṭaḥ رضي الله عنه his generous material support and financial assistance. But then Allah revealed the following verse:

وَلْيَعْفُوا۟ وَلْيَصْفَحُوٓا۟ ۗ أَلَا تُحِبُّونَ أَن يَغْفِرَ ٱللَّهُ لَكُمْ

"Let them pardon and forgive. Do you not love to be forgiven by Allah?"[93]

[93] *al-Nūr*, 24:22.

Our loved ones generally bring us great happiness and blessings, but in some cases they bring us the most pain. In the latter case, it is important to not reciprocate with the same harmful orientation. Instead, one should exercise patience and forgive them. By doing so, one will be from the elite class of believers:

وَلَمَن صَبَرَ وَغَفَرَ إِنَّ ذَٰلِكَ لَمِنْ عَزْمِ ٱلْأُمُورِ

"And whoever endures patiently and forgives—
surely this is a resolve to aspire to."[94]

Anybody can display good character when meeting and speaking with a calm and gentle person. The true test of patience arises when one is forced to speak with a foul person of evil character. In the latter circumstance, can you control your tongue and ensure that you do not utter obscene and unbecoming words? Can you maintain your pious intentions in such circumstances and continue to serve your Creator, even if you are belittled? While it is true that such antagonistic figures are evil, they have nevertheless been created in this universe for a reason and wisdom. For even the worst of tyrants cause the pious to improve their degree of patience and reliance on their Creator, thereby elevating their rewards in the afterlife. The accursed Shayṭān himself actually provides every believer the opportunity to improve their rank in front of Allah if they resist his evil whispers and temptations.

[94] *al-Shūrā*, 42:43.

Imam Ibn Qayyim al-Jawziyyah ﷺ enumerates a number of tactics and tools which a believer may employ or internalize in order to overcome a bitter experience. The first fundamental step is realizing that these experiences are divine tests, just like how other tribulations—including famine, sickness, and anxiety—are brought down to measure the faith of Allah's servants. Many Muslims are able to bear these latter conventional tribulations with patience, but when they are wronged by a fellow friend or loved one, they explode with anger and resentment. Ibn al-Qayyim ﷺ notes that it is necessary for the believer to realize that the latter is also a test from Allah ﷻ.

The second strategy that Ibn al-Qayyim ﷺ stresses is prioritizing patience over revenge. This is the case since patience guarantees immense rewards for its agent. For Allah says in the Qur'an:

إِنَّمَا يُوَفَّى ٱلصَّٰبِرُونَ أَجْرَهُم بِغَيْرِ حِسَابٍ

"Only those who endure patiently will be given their reward without limit."[95]

This Quranic verse is remarkable in its import. For while Allah ﷻ usually assigns rewards to virtuous deeds in accordance with their goodness, in this verse it is clearly stated that He grants patience unlimited rewards. Furthermore, patience's high rank can be traced to the fact that it allows its agent to attain a strong sense of inner peace

[95] *al-Zumar,* 39:10.

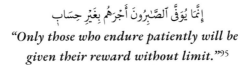

and content. This is in stark contrast to vengeance, which almost always causes its doer to go down a dark downward spiral of transgression.

The third course of action outlined by Ibn al-Qayyim ﵀ is the recognition that displaying a gentle and calm demeanour to one's wrongdoers will cause Allah ﷿ to reward His servant by showering Him with goodness despite his wrongdoings and sins. To demonstrate this point, Ibn al-Qayyim ﵀ cites the following stanza that states:

مِنْ أَجْلِكَ جَعَلْتُ خَدِّيْ أَرْضاً لِلشَّامِتِ وَالْحَسُوْدِ حَتَّى تَرْضَى

"For Your sake [O Allah], I put my cheek to the ground to the one who insults me and to the one who is envious so that You can be pleased with me."

The person who foregoes his right against the wrongdoers figuratively puts his cheek on the ground; such a posture demonstrates the highest level of humility and submission to their Creator. This explains why his Lord rewards him limitlessly and handsomely, since he debased himself out of the hope that his Creator would honour him.

The fourth step is to realize the peaceful rank of *salāmah al-ṣadr* (tranquility of the heart), whereby one frees their soul from any external acts of malice, does away with any grudges, and makes peace with the Decree of their Creator. This level of spiritual ascent may seem unfeasible for many people, since it requires a high degree of altruism and disconnection from the trappings of the temporal world. But a person can gain a strong degree of familiarity and appreciation of this spiritual degree by corresponding with individuals who were betrayed by their friends in the past but nevertheless abandoned all grudges in pursuit of the satisfaction of their Lord.

On one occasion, a man entered a gathering of the Prophet ﷺ and the latter said: "This man is a person of Paradise." 'Abdullāh ibn 'Amr ؓ was astounded to hear this, and he quickly proceeded to follow this man to his household to record all of his distinctive traits. Quite naturally, 'Abdullāh ibn 'Amr ؓ was expecting this man to be an extremely pious person who fasted during the day and performed supererogatory prayers in the night. But it soon became apparent that his intuition was incorrect, as the man did not undertake any such deeds. Instead, the only distinctive thing about him was that before sleeping every night he would empty his heart of any grudges. This emptied his heart of any distractions and satanic whispers, such that he could devote full attention to his Creator and worship with full concentration. The quality of his acts of devotion were thus extremely high, as he did not think of anything save his Creator.

Not all people have the disposition to easily give up all their grudges overnight. But over time, it is possible for them to purify their hearts and minds from such misgivings and to have their figurative wounds heal. The sacred traditions of the Islamic faith assign much assumption to the temporal dimension. After all, Allah ﷻ swears by the passage of time, and the Prophet ﷺ said that Allah is *al-Dahr* (lit. Time), which is a reference to how He created and controls time.[96] From these textual references, one can derive the key finding that the progression of time can cause virtually any spiritual wound to heal and instil tranquillity to the most disturbed soul. In this regard, one may reflect on the story of the Prophet Yūsuf عليه السلام, who was brutally betrayed by his brothers and sold for a paltry price. Despite all the dangers and threats he had to overcome in Egypt, Yūsuf's heart always remained pure and he never harboured any grudge against his brothers. In fact, his disposition untainted such that he was willing to forgive his brothers even before he met them. From this event we can learn the important lesson of always having the openness to forgive, even if the other side has not changed. In this regard, Ibn ʿAṭāʾallāh al-Iskandarī رحمه الله said:

رُبَّمَا كُنْتَ مُسِيئًا فَأَرَاكَ الإِحْسَانَ مِنْكَ صُحْبَتُكَ مَنْ هوَ أَسْوَأُ حَالًا مِنْك

"You might be in a bad state. But then your association with the one who is worse than you makes you see the virtue in yourself."

[96] See *Ṣaḥīḥ al-Bukhārī*, 4549, *Ṣaḥīḥ Muslim*, 2246.

15

What if I could have changed things?

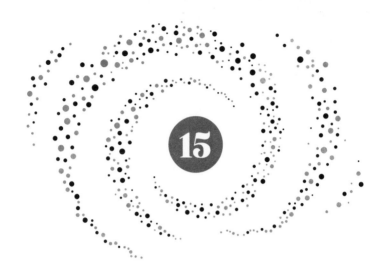

When our life takes a wrong turn, we often start invoking counterfactuals that always start with the conditional clause "if". People who are going through a dark spell say, "If only this had not happened, I would have been happy right now." The "if this, then that" construction is a regular phrase used by individuals who are dissatisfied with their current state of affairs. The believer, however, should avoid the use of the word "if", since it causes someone to dwell in the negative and surmise how their life should be instead of appreciating what they currently have. The Prophet ﷺ warned Muslims from such deliberations, since they are from the malicious devices of Shayṭān. This does not mean that the believer cannot have any regrets about their past decisions or life events, but such thoughts must only be entertained in a moderate fashion and not reflect any dissatisfaction with the divine Decree of Allah ﷻ.

One of the darkest moments in the history of the Muslim Ummah was the massacre of Karbalā', where the forces of the Umayyads killed the beloved grandson of the Prophet ﷺ. There was a man in the city of Basra who presided as a general in the army of ʿUbayd Allāh ibn Ziyād, who served Yazīd ibn Muʿāwiyah. This general narrated that on one particular day he was on his rooftop; owing to an accident he slipped, ultimately falling down on his legs. Because both of his legs were broken, he was forced to take a leave from his work and rest at home. While he was bedridden, the righteous scholar and Successor Abū Qilābah رحمه الله came to pay him a visit. The latter said to this soldier:

أَرْجُوْا أَنْ يَكُوْنَ ذَالِكَ خَيْرًا

"I hope this was actually better for you."

The soldier was surprised to hear this. In a surprised tone, he said: "What in the world could be good about my legs being broken?" But with the fullest degree of confidence, Abū Qilābah رحمه الله said:

مَا سَتَرَ اللّٰهُ عَلَيْكَ أَكْثَرُ

"What Allah protected you from if your legs were not broken is better for you."

The general remained skeptical. But he then said: "Three days later I received a letter from 'Ubayd Allāh ibn Ziyād enlisting me to join an army to go fight Ḥusayn ﵁, the grandson of the Prophet ﷺ." He responded to 'Ubayd Allāh, citing his current impairment; he was subsequently excused. Just one week later, he heard the news that this army brutally murdered Ḥusayn ﵁. The general was shocked to realize that had it not been for his injury, he would have been a part of this unjust army. He thus exclaimed:

رَحِمَ اللّٰهُ أَبَا قِلَابَةَ لَقَدْ صَدَقَ، إِنَّهُ كَانَ خِيرَةً لِي

"May Allah have mercy on Abū Qilābah. He was certainly on the mark that it was better for me."

Regret is an unavoidable dimension of human nature, since to err is human. Many of our mistakes do have long-term consequences, and as such they do warrant reflection on our part. But serious problems arise when we begin to imagine alternative realities and construct counterfactuals in our mind. During the latter scenario, the word "if" is often used, which can cause one to develop doubts and misgivings with the Divine Decree of Allah ﷻ. The Prophet ﷺ prohibited a person from entertaining counterfactuals like "If I had not done that, then this would not have happened," since such thoughts open the door of the accursed Shayṭān. Shayṭān enjoys casting doubts in the believer's mind and causing them to doubt the Wisdom and Will of Allah ﷻ, thereby causing them to exit the fold of Islam. The antidote he prescribed in such a scenario was the following:

وَلَكِنْ قُلْ قَدَّرَ اللَّهُ وَمَا شَاءَ فَعَلَ

"Instead, say: 'Allah did what He had ordained to do.'"

In his discussion on this Hadith, the famous scholar Qāḍī 'Iyāḍ ؒ said that the use of the phrase "if only" can eventually develop into a dangerous habit which will in the long run strip one's heart of *riḍā* (contentment) with Allah's Will.[97] This aforementioned discussion does not mean that all "ifs" are innately wrong. A person can learn from their past mistakes and use them as a tool to improve their future life choices. Such a process is actually praised in the Islamic ethos, and is known as *muḥāsabah* (accountability). Evaluating one's past errors and learning from them is a central aspect behind a person's spiritual development. The Prophet ﷺ himself used this type of introspective process with his Companions.

97 Qāḍī 'Iyāḍ, *Mashāriq al-Anwār 'alā Ṣiḥāḥ al-Āthār*, vol. 1, p. 364.

The believer's disposition is always grateful and positive, since they look at the "ifs" that went towards their favour in this world, which in turn cause them to be more thankful to their Lord.

For instance, while he was performing Hajj, he said:

وَلَوْلاَ أَنَّ مَعِي الْهَدْيَ لأَحْلَلْتُ

"If only I would not have brought my sacrificial animal with me, I would have exited my state of iḥrām."[98]

These types of statements are valuable and are of rich pedagogical value; through them, Muslim scholars have been able to derive a myriad of legal rulings. In addition, a person may make such a statement in order to indicate their regret at being unable to perform a good deed. In this regard, Imam al-Nawawī ﷺ said:

أَمَّا مَنْ قَالَهَا تَأَسُّفًا عَلَى مَا فَاتَ مِنْ طَاعَةِ اللّٰهِ تَعَالَى أَوْ مَا هُوَ مُتَعَذِّرٌ عَلَيْهِ مِنْ ذَلِكَ وَنَحْوَ هَذَا فَلاَ بَأْسَ بِهِ

"As for the one who says it (i.e. "If only…") because they missed out on a way of obeying Allah, the inability to perform a righteous act, or similar, then there is no harm in that."[99]

Similarly, after relating the story of Mūsā and Khiḍr ﷺ, the Prophet ﷺ said:

وَدِدْنَا أَنَّ مُوسَى كَانَ صَبَرَ حَتَّى يُقَصَّ اللّٰهُ عَلَيْنَا مِنْ خَبَرِهِمَا

"We would have loved if Mūsā was a bit more patient, so that Allah would have told us more of their stories."[100]

98 *Sunan Abī Dāwūd*, 1789.

99 al-Nawawī, *Sharḥ Ṣāḥīḥ Muslim*, vol. 16, p. 216.

100 *Ṣaḥīḥ al-Bukhārī*, 3401.

There are also "ifs" of gratitude, by which one reflects on the multitude of ways that their life could have taken a wrong turn, yet it was Allah ﷻ Who saved them from pestilence and misfortune. This is a praiseworthy type of hypothetical speech, and is often used in the Qur'an. For instance, Allah ﷻ states in the Qur'an:

وَلَوْلَا فَضْلُ ٱللَّهِ عَلَيْكُمْ وَرَحْمَتُهُۥ فِى ٱلدُّنْيَا وَٱلْءَاخِرَةِ
لَمَسَّكُمْ فِى مَآ أَفَضْتُمْ فِيهِ عَذَابٌ عَظِيمٌ

"Had it not been for Allah's Grace and Mercy upon you in this world and the Hereafter, you would have certainly been touched with a tremendous punishment for what you plunged into."[101]

Likewise, in another Quranic verse, we find the following statement from a person who is saved in the Hereafter and enters Paradise:

وَلَوْلَا نِعْمَةُ رَبِّي لَكُنْتُ مِنَ الْمُحْضَرِينَ

"Had it not been for the Grace of my Lord, I would have certainly been among those brought [to Hell]."[102]

The believer's disposition is always grateful and positive, since they look at the "ifs" that went towards their favour in this world, which in turn cause them to be more thankful to their Lord. From this fact, one can derive a fundamental principle

101 *al-Nūr,* 24:14.

102 *al-Ṣāffāt,* 37:57.

of life: one should only engage in hypotheticals when looking at their blessings, not at their losses and tragedies. With reference to this matter, Ibn ʿAṭāʾallāh al-Iskandarī ﵀ said:

مَتَى فَتَحَ لَكَ بابَ الفَهْمِ فِي المَنْعِ، عَادَ المَنْعُ عَيْنَ العَطَاء

"When He opens up your understanding of deprivation, the deprivation itself becomes the same as a gift."

There will be points in this life where one will be dissatisfied with the path that they are currently placed on, but they should realize that this is the Decree of their Lord. Attempting to fight or resist against it will never bring peace and tranquillity. The solution is to display contentment and submission to the Creator. In this regard, Imam al-Shāfiʿī ﵀ said: "My heart is at ease knowing that what was meant for me will never miss me and what has missed me was never meant for me." Thus, instead of engaging with spiritually damaging "ifs" one should look at what currently is, that is, the current benedictions that their Lord has provided them.

16

Why do they get the life I want?

On many occasions, one may feel that they have the shorter end of the stick in life. A person may come from a disadvantaged background and exert impressive efforts to improve their circumstances, but the objective external conditions around them hold them back. Meanwhile, they find that someone else with a relatively easier background is able to have the life that they always wanted. This may be a frustrating sight for a person, which ultimately causes them to ask: "Why is success granted for others, but not for me?"

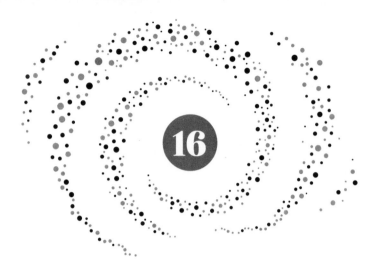

The Companion Ibn Masʿūd ﷺ provided the answer to this question in an incredible narration, in which he states:

إِنَّ الْعَبْدَ لَيَهُمُّ بِالْأَمْرِ مِنَ التِجَارَةِ وَالْإِمَارَةِ حَتَّى يُيَسَرَ لَهُ

"A servant will continuously be engaged in an affair of this world, such as trade or political leadership, until it becomes easy for them."

This servant comes at the cusp of their desired life goal, and its retrieval appears to be inevitable. But then, Ibn Masʿūd ﷺ continues, Allah ﷻ may wish to divert it from them for a higher objective:

فَيَنْظُرُ اللهُ إِلَيْهِ، فَيَقُوْلُ لِلْمَلَائِكَةِ اِصْرِفُوْهُ عَنْهُ فَإِنْ يَسَّرْتُه لَه أَدْخَلْتُه النَّارَ

"[Allah looks at him and says to the Angels:] 'Divert it away from him. For if I were to give him this blessing, then I will have to put him in the Hellfire.'"

In His rationale for taking away this blessing, Allah ﷻ mentions that its retrieval will push this servant to fall into heedlessness and abandon a morally upright lifestyle, ultimately causing them to lose in the Hereafter. The servant does not know this long-term reality, and looks at their loss from a purely this-worldly perspective:

فَيَصْرِفُه عَنْهُ فَيَظَلُّ يَتَطَيَّرُ يَقُوْلُ سَبَقَنِيْ فُلَانٌ، وَأَهَانَنِيْ فُلَانٌ،
وَمَا هُوَ إِلَّا فَضْلُ اللهِ عَزَّ وَ جَلَّ عَلَيْه

"It will be taken away from him, which will cause him to continuously say, 'So-and-so beat me to it; this person got

the position or the possessions that I thought I was going to get.' But during this entire process it was nothing but Allah's blessing upon him." [103]

Perhaps the most striking portion of this narration is where the servant sees the worldly benefit he craved being withheld and given to another person. This causes him to feel frustrated, such that he may become convinced that someone interfered with their Divine Decree and stole from them something that was rightfully theirs. The sensation of frustration and anger can be compounded if the other person is a hostile figure that meted an injustice against them in the past. This all causes the person to ask why someone else is living the life they deserve.

Throughout human history, there have been righteous and upright individuals deserving of a relatively comfortable lifestyle yet they were forced to endure countless difficulties and struggles. On the other hand, there have been malicious and malevolent figures who were granted lives of ease and comfort notwithstanding the injustices and wrongs that they meted against others. The Muslim living in the present should take this fact into account, and realize that even if they give charity generously, stand for that which is upright and moral, and support the oppressed, they may not be recompensed for their righteous acts in this world.

---

103 Ibn Rajab al-Ḥanbalī, *Jāmiʿ al-ʿUlūm wa al-Ḥikam*, vol. 2, p. 559.

From an Islamic perspective, looking at the "winners" of this world with anger and frustration is wrong for two reasons. First and foremost, such an outlook inevitably leads to jealousy and envy, which is prohibited in Islam. It is reported that the Prophet ﷺ said:

إِيَّاكُمْ وَالْحَسَدَ فَإِنَّ الْحَسَدَ يَأْكُلُ الْحَسَنَاتِ كَمَا تَأْكُلُ النَّارُ الْحَطَبَ

"Beware of envy, for verily it burns one's good deeds the way that fire burns through wood."

Jealousy causes a person's inner spirit and temperament to be burned by a raging fire, which can in the long run lead to physical and emotional problems. But another equally important reason why it is incorrect to look at the blessings of others with disdain is that the vision of humans are short-sighted and reductionist; just like how many of our hardships have blessings, many of the blessings granted to others be embedded with numerous hardships. For instance, the blessings that are granted to people of evil are actually distractions that will inevitably spell their end. In this regard, Allah ﷻ states:

فَلَا تُعْجِبْكَ أَمْوَالُهُمْ وَلَا أَوْلَادُهُمْ إِنَّمَا يُرِيدُ اللَّهُ لِيُعَذِّبَهُم بِهَا

"So let neither their wealth nor children impress you [O Prophet]. Allah only intends to torment them through these things in this worldly life."[104]

104 *al-Tawbah*, 9:55.

The worldly benefits given to such people are only superficial and external, since they are devoid of any *barakah* (blessings). They may outwardly appear to have it all, but in reality they are spiritually empty and devoid of any happiness. In the long run, their wealth will become the source of their pain. Their children will become their own enemies and enforce upon them the same brutality and harshness that they imposed upon others. This in fact mirrors the story of the oppressors: while they are indulging in the vain pleasures and distractions of this material world, they will face a sudden and painful downfall.

Undoubtedly, it is difficult for the believers to see the oppressors and wrongdoers walk freely in this world, whereby they continue to exert their influence in an apparently unabated fashion. For instance, it must have been difficult for the Companion ʿAmmār ibn Yāsir ﵁ to see Abū Jahl—who had mercilessly killed his parents—in Mecca on a daily basis. But for ʿAmmār ﵁ and other oppressed believers, the following Quranic verse was their source of relief:

وَٱلْعَٰقِبَةُ لِلْمُتَّقِينَ

"The ultimate outcome belongs to the righteous."[105]

The final victory thus belongs to the believers and the people of piety. It is important to note that the people who are allowed to enjoy the bounties, wealth, and pleasures of this world are not necessarily evil folk. They may be Muslims,

---

105 *al-Qaṣaṣ*, 28:83.

The reality of this world is that the material and physical pleasures are overrated, as they are fleeting and transient. Search for the spiritual roots of happiness, and you will reap eternal rewards in the Hereafter.

but their faith and conviction is weaker than the righteous folk deprived of such successes in this world. In other words, Allah ﷻ may be giving the former a greater share of this world, but the true bounties of the afterlife are assigned to the latter. When compared to the Hereafter, the successes and recognition of this world are worthless.

This moral lesson is most greatly articulated in the story of the Anṣār, who sacrificed their lives and wealth to serve the blessed Prophet ﷺ and the message of Islam. After inviting the Prophet ﷺ to the city of Medina and submitting to his leadership, the Anṣār participated in a number of military expeditions to thwart the attacks of the polytheists. Through their constant resolve and service, they were able to the facilitate the conquest of Mecca. Naturally, through their many years of service the Anṣār expected to be materially rewarded for their efforts, especially at the Battle of Ḥunayn, which marked the complete defeat of the polytheists. But much to their surprise, the Prophet ﷺ gave all the spoils of war to the recent converts of Islam, many of whom were—just a few months prior—some of the most hostile enemies of the Islamic faith. The Anṣār were hurt with this course of action, since they felt that the Prophet ﷺ had assigned precedence to the people of Mecca, and would likely leave Medina in the near future. The Prophet ﷺ sensed their disappointment and comforted them by stating: "Are you not pleased, O Anṣār, that these people go home with their wealth and camels, but you go back to Medina and you have the Messenger of Allah with you?" This statement raised the hearts and spirits of the

Anṣār, since it reminded them that salvation in the afterlife is the true yardstick of success. The assurances of the Prophet ﷺ that he would stay with them in Medina gave them peace of mind and caused them to forget the pain of being deprived the spoils of war.

It is reported that the great Companion ʿUbādah ibn al-Ṣāmit رضي الله عنه said to his son:

يَا بُنَيَّ، إِنَّكَ لَنْ تَجِدَ طَعْمَ حَقِيقَةِ الْإِيمَانِ حَتَّى تَعْلَمَ أَنَّ مَا أَصَابَكَ
لَمْ يَكُنْ لِيُخْطِئَكَ، وَمَا أَخْطَأَكَ لَمْ يَكُنْ لِيُصِيبَكَ

"O my son, you will never truly taste the sweetness of faith until you know that what has come to you was never meant to miss you and that which has missed you was never destined to come to you."

Echoing this sentiment, Imam Ibn Qayyim al-Jawziyyah رحمه الله said:

لَا بُدَّ مِنْ نُفُوذِ الْقَدْرِ فَاجْنَحْ لِلسِّلْمِ

"The Divine Decree is bound to happen, so make peace with it."

The problem with many individuals is that they fail to appreciate the many ways in which the Divine Decree works in their favour. Instead, they get tied to the specifics of what they desire and wish to acquire in this world. For instance, if they are unable to get married to a specific person, they may remain unsatisfied and angry for the rest of the their life, failing to appreciate the fact that Allah ﷻ made it possible for them to enjoy the love and companionship of someone else. It is of course acceptable for a person to ask Allah ﷻ for particular blessings where in attributes or form, but they should always be open to the possibility that Allah ﷻ has a better plan for them. Having trust in Allah's ability to open an infinite number of doors is imperative:

وَيَرْزُقْهُ مِنْ حَيْثُ لَا يَحْتَسِبُ

"And [He] provides for them from sources they could never imagine." [106]

In one of his golden aphorisms, Ibn 'Aṭā'allāh al-Iskandarī رحمه الله said:

إِنَّمَا جَعَلَهَا مَحَلاً لِلأَغْيَارِ وَمَعْدِناً لِوُجُودِ الأَكْدَارِ تَزْهِيداً لَكَ فِيهَا

"He has only made it (i.e. the world) a place of others and a mine for troubles so that you would not love it and you realize what provision beyond it awaits you."

The believer should always repeat and rely on the verse:

أَلَيْسَ ٱللَّهُ بِكَافٍ عَبْدَهُ

"Is Allah not sufficient for His servant?" [107]

106 *al-Ṭalāq*, 65:3.

107 *al-Zumar*, 39:36.

In his commentary on this verse, Imam al-Ghazālī رحمه الله says: "Is Allah not enough for his servant? For the one who has Allah will feel like he has everything and the one who does not have Allah will feel like he has nothing." At the present moment, through your prayer, recitation of the Qur'an, and visitation of the houses of Allah ﷻ, you may be enjoying a life of tranquillity that another person is lacking. The reality of this world is that the material and physical pleasures are overrated, as they are fleeting and transient. Search for the spiritual roots of happiness, and you will reap eternal rewards in the Hereafter.

قُل لَّن يُصِيبَنَا إِلَّا
مَا كَتَبَ اللَّهُ لَنَا هُوَ مَوْلَانَا
وَعَلَى اللَّهِ فَلْيَتَوَكَّلِ الْمُؤْمِنُونَ

Say, "Nothing will ever befall us except what Allah has destined for us. He is our Protector." So in Allah let the believers put their trust.

AL-TAUBAH, 51

17

I did not mean to hurt you

What happens when the oppressed realizes that they might have all along been the oppressor? For many years, a person may believe that they were wronged and abused by another individual. But as they mature physically and intellectually with the passage of time, there may come the realization that they themselves were the wrongdoer, and the other party was the victim. Such a shift in opinion is a divine gift that causes a person to evaluate their deeds and amend any potential wrongs that involved another party. There is a powerful Hadith which emphasizes this very theme; it famously relates the story of three men who were trapped in a cave after a giant boulder sealed its entry point.

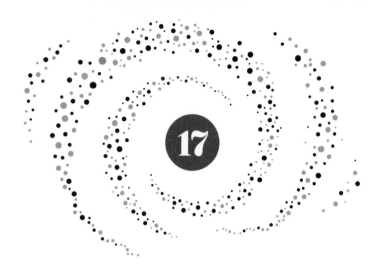

These three men became so worried by their plight that they decided to engage in intensive *du'ā'* (supplication) so that Allah ﷻ may remove them from their plight. The second man made an intimate plea to Allah ﷻ, and related a very emotional story with another figure that he was emotionally attached to. In one key segment of his invocation, he said:

اللَّهُمَّ إنَّه كانَتْ لِيَ ابْنَةُ عَمٍّ أَحْبَبْتُها كَأَشَدِّ ما يُحِبُّ
الرِّجَالُ النِّسَاءَ، وَطَلَبْتُ إِلَيْهَا نَفْسَهَا، فأبَتْ

"O Allah, I had a cousin of mine that I fell in love with and I loved her deeper than any man could love any woman. I asked her to be with me, but she refused."

This woman feared Allah ﷻ and refused to engage in unlawful sexual intercourse with her cousin. But soon a famine struck their locality, which caused her to agree to his demand out of desperation: "At some point she went into deep debt. I manipulated her by taking advantage of her desperation and telling her, 'I will give you a hundred dinars if you do what I want you to do.' So she agreed in her desperation." The man then approached his cousin in order to perform what he had been seeking all along:

فَلَمَّا وَقَعْتُ بيْنَ رِجْلَيْهَا، قالَتْ: يا عَبْدَ اللهِ اتَّقِ اللَّهَ، وَلَا تَفْتَحِ الخَاتَمَ إلَّا بحَقِّهِ، فَقُمْتُ
عَنْهَا، فإنْ كُنْتَ تَعْلَمُ أَنِّي فَعَلْتُ ذلكَ ابْتِغَاءَ وَجْهِكَ، فَافْرُجْ لَنَا منها فُرْجَةً، فَفَرَجَ لهمْ

"Just as I was about to commit that deed and I had her exactly where I wanted her at that moment, she shouted and said, 'O slave of Allah, fear Allah and do not break a seal for which He has not given you permission.' I thus got up

and I ran away. O Allah, if I did that for Your sake alone, remove this boulder. So Allah granted them relief."

This powerful story calls for much reflection. This man was stuck inside a cave and undoubtedly felt entombed. When narrating this story, he likely realized that his own cousin felt trapped due to the ordeal he tried to put her in. But it was his spiritual awakening and spark of moral consciousness which caused him to take another path that was centred around Allah ﷻ. His choice to turn away from committing an enormity undoubtedly had a positive effect in changing the course of his life and that of his cousin. This empathy is what caused his *duʿā'* to be accepted.

Unfortunately, this type of empathy and introspection is often lacking among the common masses. It is rare for a person to see a life event through another person's point of view, let alone for them to consider how their actions affected that individual's life trajectory. However, it is imperative for one to note that just as other people are a test for us, we likewise can be a trial and test for them. In this day and age, it is common for people to worry about the spiritual harms that they may absorb from other people, such as hypocrisy and immorality. Yet, the Companions ﷺ adopted a completely different standpoint in this matter: they were far more concerned about how their potential spiritual harms would affect others, since they were acutely aware of the fact that harming someone else in this world means harming oneself in the Hereafter, as such debts would have to be settled.

They preferred to be the receiver of harm in this world, since it would translate to the retrieval of rewards in the Afterlife. This is why the Prophet ﷺ once said: "Be the slave of Allah that is murdered, not the one who murders." In other words, being the wronged slave is superior to being the wronging one. This latter fact explains why Ḥasan al-Baṣrī ﵀ once said: "The eye of the hypocrite always looks outwards, whereas the eye of the believer always looks inwards." In the Qur'an, Allah ﷻ states that the hypocrites suffer from the following malady:

يَحْسَبُونَ كُلَّ صَيْحَةٍ عَلَيْهِمْ

"They think every cry is against them." [108]

This points to the insecurity of the hypocrites. They read every reminder or admonition to denote a point of criticism against them, even if it was not actually directed against them per se, and reply aggressively to their interlocutor. In stark contrast, the believers do not take any offence to such statements, and reflect on their sins and shortcomings. Even if the other party imparts words of advice in a harsh manner, the believer listens and benefits from the import of the message. Even when engaging with a hostile party, they ensure that the tone of their voice is moderate and that they do not use offensive language.

108 *al-Munāfiqūn*, 63:4.

As Muslims, we should aim to follow the path of our pious predecessors by evaluating any of our potential past misdeeds and trying to rectify them in any way possible through repentance and the commission of good deeds.

On the Day of Judgement, the detailed mechanics of every relationship will be revealed and exposed in elaborate detail. If we always portray or picture ourselves as being the victim, there is an acute danger that we will overlook the harms that we have caused to others. A person must engage in deep rounds of introspection to determine who they have potentially harmed in this world and seek to make amends, lest they be held accountable in the Hereafter. The one who fails to see his acts of wrongdoing in this world and does not take proactive action to address them will be forced to transfer their good deeds to the oppressed parties on the Day of Judgement. This could potentially leave them morally bankrupt in the sight of Allah ﷻ and jeopardize their prospects in attaining salvation.

While there are few people who have the capacity to silently admit that they erred, there are even fewer individuals in the world who have the strength and honesty to publicly proclaim to their colleagues that they were in the wrong. This is particularly the case if they had held the false notion that they were the oppressed party. But to be a righteous believers means correcting such injustices. The great scholar Wahb ibn Munabbih ؓ said that the righteous folk have three praiseworthy qualities. First and foremost, they are blessed with what is known as *sakhāwah al-nafs* (having a generous soul), such that they always have an open heart and disposition towards others. The second is *al-ṣabr ʿalā al-adhā* (exercising patience in the face of harms), where one does not let the harms and afflictions meted by others cause them to reciprocate in the same fashion. The last key element identified by Imam Ibn Munabbih ﷺ is *ṭayyib al-kalām* (being pleasant in speech), whereby one only speaks good and refrains from using any foul words in their interactions. The person who combines such qualities not only will attain rewards in the Hereafter, but they will also be able to acquire a respectable rank in this world as well.

If you have been a person who has failed to embody these praiseworthy qualities in your day-to-day conduct, a change in state is still possible. By apologizing, making amends, and repenting to Allah ﷻ, it is possible for one's worst of enemies to become sincere companions and friends. There were several figures in the early Islamic period who had committed wrongs against the Prophet ﷺ and the Companions ﷺ, but they then submitted to his call, repented, and became morally upright individuals. For example, Waḥshī killed Ḥamzah ﷺ—the beloved uncle of the Prophet ﷺ—in the Battle of Uḥud with a spear. After accepting Islam, he was immensely regretful for his deed, but he knew that the past could not be changed. He instead sought to use his skills to serve Islam, and ended up using the same spear to kill the enemy of Islam, Musaylimah. In a similar fashion, Saʿīd ibn ʿĀmir ﷺ was once an enemy of Islam, and was present during the brutal execution of Khubayb ibn ʿAdī ﷺ. After accepting Islam, he was horrified by his participation in this affair, but he knew that he could not reverse what had occurred many years prior. But he exerted his best and most genuine efforts to serve Islam as a faithful administrator in the Levant region. As Muslims, we should aim to follow the path of our pious predecessors by evaluating any of our potential past misdeeds and trying to rectify them in any way possible through repentance and the commission of good deeds. Ibn ʿAṭāʾallāh al-Iskandarī ﵀ said:

تَشَوُّفُكَ إِلَى مَا بَطَنَ فِيكَ مِنَ العُيُوبِ خَيْرٌ مِنْ
تَشَوُّفِكَ إِلى مَا حُجِبَ عَنْكَ مِنَ الغُيوبِ

"Your being on the lookout for the vices hidden within you is far better than your being on the lookout for the invisible realities that have been veiled from you."

قُل لَّن يُصِيبَنَا إِلَّا مَا كَتَبَ ٱللَّهُ لَنَا هُوَ مَوْلَىٰنَا
وَعَلَى ٱللَّهِ فَلْيَتَوَكَّلِ ٱلْمُؤْمِنُونَ

Say, "Nothing will ever befall us except what Allah has destined for us. He is our Protector." So in Allah let the believers put their trust.

AL-TAUBAH, 51

18

How do I find love in loneliness?

This world is full of countless individuals and people, with every figure having their own unique personality and temperament. Despite this sheer diversity, you are still single and without a companion. In the backdrop of such loneliness, you are depressed and dissatisfied with life. How does one come to terms with such solitude, and is there a way to break away from its vicious cycles?

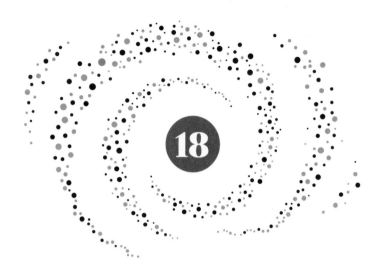

Humans naturally crave communal ties and developing bonds with others. In fact, one of the roots for the word *insān* (human) is *uns*, which refers to the comfort that one acquires due to keeping company with others. For this reason, it is no surprise to find many scholars state that humans are social beings, which is why they live in communities and societies. This also explains why the prophetic Sunnah has legislated a myriad of community activities. For instance, the Prophet ﷺ urged his followers—especially men—to perform the five prayers in the mosque; during Ramadan, these intra-communal ties are even further intensified through the performance of the special *tarāwīḥ* prayers in the night. For the daily meals, the Prophet ﷺ urged family members and community members to eat together in the same setting. When travelling, the Prophet ﷺ urged a person to always have a companion; in fact, in some narrations he forbade people from spending the night by oneself or travelling alone.[109] He explained these aforementioned directives by stating: "Shayṭān is like a wolf that always attacks the lone sheep. So stay close to the community and do not isolate yourself."

Even in special family events, Islam encourages the invitation of community members. For instance, after having conducted the marriage contract, one is recommended to have a *walīmah* (wedding banquet). In addition, after one has a newborn child, they are recommended to hold a special *ʿaqīqah* ceremony. On a similar note, the Prophet ﷺ praised circles of knowledge and remembrance, mentioning that they embody the gardens of Paradise and are attended by the Angels close to Allah ﷻ.

---

109 *Musnad Imām Aḥmad*, 5650.

Allah ﷻ created all beings in pairs:

وَمِن كُلِّ شَيْءٍ خَلَقْنَا زَوْجَيْنِ لَعَلَّكُمْ تَذَكَّرُونَ

"And We created pairs of all things so perhaps you would be mindful."[110]

This divine imperative was exemplified by the Prophets ﷺ. For instance, Mūsā ﷺ asked Allah ﷻ to make his brother Hārūn ﷺ his aide, that is, as a fellow Prophet:

اشْدُدْ بِهِ أَزْرِي وَأَشْرِكْهُ فِي أَمْرِي

"Strengthen me through him, and let him share my task."[111]

In light of this grand request, some exegetes and commentators have stated that no person has granted another figure a greater favour than Mūsā ﷺ, for it was through his prayer that his brother became a Prophet. Mūsā ﷺ made this prayer due to the loneliness he felt in spreading the divine message of Islam to Firʿawn and his wicked supporters. In a similar fashion, humans feel incomplete when they are isolated, and ultimately crave for a spouse to provide them comfort and perfect their physical and spiritual disposition. In one key Quranic verse, Allah ﷻ states:

وَمِنْ آيَاتِهِ أَنْ خَلَقَ لَكُم مِّنْ أَنفُسِكُمْ أَزْوَاجًا لِّتَسْكُنُوا إِلَيْهَا وَجَعَلَ بَيْنَكُم مَّوَدَّةً وَرَحْمَةً ۚ إِنَّ فِي ذَٰلِكَ لَآيَاتٍ لِّقَوْمٍ يَتَفَكَّرُونَ

110 *al-Dhāriyāt*, 51:49.

111 *Ṭā Hā*, 20:31-31.

"And one of His signs is that He created for you spouses from
among yourselves so that you may find comfort in them.
And He has placed between you compassion and mercy.
Surely in this are signs for people who reflect."[112]

Regarding the portion of the verse "and He has placed
between you compassion and mercy", Imam al-Rāzī 🙏 made
a beautiful observation concerning the signs of the Divine in
marriage. He said that after marrying their spouse, a person
can have more love for them—within the short span of a few
months—than the family they lived with throughout their
life. But undoubtedly, the best marriage unions are those in
which the two families of the parties come together, such that
the rights and ranks of every person is respected and no one is
forgotten and secluded. Instead, the circle of love and mercy
grows and supports the two parties in their spiritual journey.

In Paradise, there is no notion of loneliness, as every soul will
be given a beautiful spouse who will accompany them for all
of eternity. If they were married in this temporal world and
both attain salvation, then they will be united in Paradise to
share even more beautiful moments in the abode of bliss. But
what if someone is destined to remain lonely in this world,
and they do not end up being granted a loving spouse or any
type of meaningful friendship?

---

[112] *al-Rūm*, 30:21.

The scholars have stated that there are multiple forms and layers of loneliness. The first is where one is without any family member or friend due to external circumstances. Undoubtedly, such an experience may be difficult for a person, but it could in the long run unlock the spiritual benefits found in the practice of *khalwah* (religious seclusion), whereby one is able to develop a close and intimate relationship with their Creator without the obstruction of any distractions.

But there is another category of loneliness which is even harder than the aforementioned one, namely the separation borne from estrangement. During the course of your life, there will be people who will opt to break ties with you owing to schisms or tensions that emerge over time. Sometimes, this disunity may stem from your own problematic behaviour, such as you exercising poor conduct in the presence of others. Such an action is undoubtedly blameworthy, and the fact that it leads to these types of consequences is understandable. After all, the Prophet ﷺ said that the worst of people are those who are abandoned by others, since no one wishes to engage with their foul mouths. If you have been abandoned by your family and peers for this reason, it may be that Allah ﷻ desires for you to address their spiritual and behavioural ills so that you may be a productive and healthy member of society once again.

Quite paradoxically, in other cases the cause of estrangement may actually be positive. This is when a person strives to perform good deeds and sets higher standards of moral conduct upon themselves. This type of behaviour sometimes causes one's friends to find their associate to be "extreme" and "too religious", which in turns leads to a praiseworthy form of estrangement that is known as *ghurbah*. In his commentary on this state, Ibn Qayyim al-Jawziyyah states that loneliness is not in and of itself a spiritual rank. But when a person rises in their station, loneliness is often a byproduct that is decreed by the Divine. For as he puts it:

أَلْعَارِفُ أَنِسٍ بِاللهِ أَوْحَشَه مِنْ غَيْرِه

"The knower of Allah finds closeness to Him, which causes him to distance himself from other than Him."[113]

Thus, both good and bad deeds can cause a person to be decreed with loneliness and estrangement. But regardless of whatever the cause may be, a person should not let this loneliness go to waste. It should be employed as a learning moment whereby one aspires to find Allah. In a famous Hadith Qudsī, Allah says:

أَنَا عِنْدَ ظَنِّ عَبْدِي بِي، وَأَنَا مَعَهُ إِذَا ذَكَرَنِي، فَإِن ذَكَرَنِي فِي نَفْسِهِ،
ذَكَرْتُهُ فِي نَفسي، وإِنْ ذَكَرَنِي فِي ملإٍ، ذكرتُهُ في ملإٍ خَيْرٍ منهم

"I am what My servant thinks of Me, and I am with him when he remembers Me. If he remembers Me in himself, I will remember him in Myself. And if he remembers Me in a gathering, I make mention of him in a greater gathering than his."

---

113 Ibn al-Qayyim, *Rawḍah al-Muḥibbīn,* p. 552.

This Hadith is momentous in its import and indicates that loneliness has endless spiritual openings. For when Allah ﷻ decrees that His servant be deprived of his worldly *rizq* (provision) and the latter accepts this trial with patience, Allah ﷻ will grant them greater material gifts in the afterlife. But when Allah ﷻ decrees that His servant be afflicted with loneliness and he accepts this test with beautiful perseverance, Allah ﷻ will grant them the greatest gift conceivable: Himself. This point was beautifully encapsulated by Ibn ʿAṭāʾallāh al-Iskandarī ﷺ in the following aphorism:

مَتى أَوْحَشَكَ مِنْ خَلْقِهِ فَاعْلَمْ أَنَّهُ يُرِيدُ أَنْ يَفْتَحَ لَكَ بابَ الأُنْسِ بِهِ

"When He alienates you from His creatures, then know that He wants to open for you the door of intimacy with Him."

Thus, the believer can and must always welcome divine trials and tests with endurance and a positive disposition. Loneliness is undoubtably a challenging experience, but diagnosing the reasons behind its emergence is necessary to see whether it could be changed or overcame. If it stems from poor conduct, one should make amends and seek forgiveness from the negatively affected parties. If it is due to one's positive change and improved conduct as a Muslim, then they should be pleased to know that Allah ﷻ wishes to elevate their status as a special friend.

Both good and bad deeds can cause a person to be decreed with loneliness and estrangement. But regardless of whatever the cause may be, this loneliness should be employed as a learning moment whereby one aspires to find Allah ﷻ.

19

Why did they have to die?

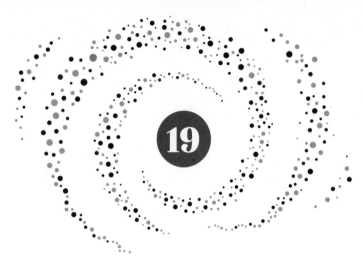

In a famous Hadith Qudsī, Allah ﷿ states: "I do not hesitate about anything as much as I hesitate about seizing the soul of My faithful servant. For he hates death and I hate to disappoint him." Yet, such an event is not just disappointing; in fact, it could be totally destructive for all the family members that have been left behind. Such a loss can be especially painful if the household was at the cusp of enjoying material and spiritual stability. But this should not lead to the end of hope, for a person's relationship with a loved one can actually strengthen after they die, since there are a myriad of ways available to support them. For example, after their passing one enjoys the golden opportunity to perform good deeds on their behalf, something which was not possible when they were still alive.

After a loved one passes away, a person's life will undoubtedly never be the same. Throughout his life the blessed Prophet ﷺ had to see and experience the death of many of his close loved ones, which led to much pain and grief. He had to personally bury many of his immediate family members, such as his beloved wife Khadījah ؓ and six of his seven children. His father passed away before he was even born, which meant that he was raised as an orphan. In addition, he had to bury his mother and his grandfather when he was six and nine years old respectively. When he was going through a difficult crisis, his supporter and paternal uncle Abū Ṭālib passed away.

When grieving for the loss of his loved ones, the conduct of the Messenger of Allah was profoundly human yet also perfectly prophetic at the same time. Perhaps the most touching and sentimental event in this regard is when his son Ibrāhīm passed away. As he held his deceased son in his lap and his tears rapidly fell, the Prophet ﷺ said: "The eyes shed tears and the heart grieves, and we are hurting over your loss, O Ibrāhīm. But we will not say except that which pleases our Lord." The Prophet ﷺ did not have any doubts that Ibrāhīm would go to Paradise, but he was still tremendously hurt due to his son's departure from this world. In his interaction with his deceased son during this touching moment, the Prophet ﷺ exemplified perfect levels of *raḥmah* (mercy) and *riḍā* (contentment). In his discussion on these two values, Ibn al-Qayyim ﷺ states that when reacting to a tragedy, a person can demonstrate varying levels of *raḥmah* and *riḍā*. The highest is when one has perfect levels of both, whereby one is touched by the tragedy and cries, but their heart is fully content with Allah's Will. The level below that is when a person has *raḥmah* but lacks *riḍā*; in this scenario, a person grieves for their loss, but they lack any contentment in their heart. The third level is when a person has *riḍā* but no *raḥmah*; such a person abstractly accepts the divine Will of Allah ﷻ, but is not emotionally moved by the event. Then there is the lowest level, where one has no *raḥmah* and *riḍā*, whereby they display resentment to the Divine Decree and mourn without any limit.[114]

Undoubtedly, the Prophet ﷺ perfectly encompassed these two values in the face of a tragedy, and he illustrated both of them in a balanced fashion. Other figures could not undertake such a thing. For instance, Ibn Taymiyyah ﷺ was once asked about how some great Muslim scholars did not cry when they lost a family member, despite them exercising *riḍā*. In other words, they were content with Allah's Decree, but lacked the emotional beauty found in the Prophet ﷺ. In this regard, one may consider the case of al-Fuḍayl ibn ʿIyāḍ ﷺ, who attended the funeral of his son Yūsuf with a noticeable smile on his face. This sight surprised the onlookers, who ultimately asked al-Fuḍayl ﷺ if he was indeed grieving. Al-

114 Ibn al-Qayyim, *Madārij al-Sālikīn*, p. 203.

Fuḍayl ﵀ responded to them by saying: "I wanted to show Allah that I accept his Divine Decree." Ibn Taymiyyah ﵀ was ultimately asked whether al-Fuḍayl's response was superior to that of the Prophet ﷺ. Ibn Taymiyyah ﵀ responded by stating that undoubtedly the response of the Prophet ﷺ was superior, since he did not need to curb his *raḥmah* in order to manifest his *riḍā*. On the other hand, al-Fuḍayl ﵀ had to restrain any manifestation of mercy or emotional pity to maintain his contentment, so his reaction was weaker.

People can spiritually outlive the divine limits that are imposed on their biological clock, but this depends on the measures that their loved ones and family members take after their death. Any form of goodness or teaching that they imparted should be cherished and passed on to others in order to amplify their scale of righteous deeds. That way, notwithstanding their death they will continue to rise in rank and their actions will many future generations to come on this Earth.

Besides aiding the deceased through the transference of good deeds in their name, one should also aim to be a source of comfort for one's fellow family members and loved ones who have been afflicted with the same loss. Providing them moral support is a highly praiseworthy deed, and will allow all the afflicted parties to overcome the tragedy and collectively heal. As for the deceased party, Allah ﷿ blesses the living family members with a myriad of memories and golden moments in the past, all of which should be shared and cherished. Even after death, the loved ones and relatives of the deceased can construct new memories by giving charity on their behalf and making supplications for their safety and salvation in the Hereafter. As an extension of this rule, sometimes people learn certain beautiful facts and secrets about their loved ones only after they have passed away, such as them performing acts of charity in the night or regularly engaging in a special act of worship at a point of the day.

But perhaps the greatest blessing is that Allah ﷻ may decree Paradise for the living family members if they are patient with the death of their loved one. In another striking Hadith Qudsī, Allah ﷻ is reported as stating:

مَا لِعَبْدِي الْمُؤْمِنِ عِنْدِي جَزَاءٌ، إِذَا قَبَضْتُ صَفِيَّهُ مِنْ أَهْلِ الدُّنْيَا، ثُمَّ احْتَسَبَهُ إِلاَّ الْجَنَّةُ

"I have nothing to give but Paradise as a reward to My believing servant who—if I cause their loved one to die—remains patient."

This divine rule applies not just for our direct family members, but any deceased person that we happened to love. In all such cases, Allah ﷻ is well aware of how much we loved such illustrious figures during our lifetimes and thus will reward us for our patience with the eternal gardens and bounties of Paradise. Being able to patiently accept such tragedies and handle such difficulties by relying on Allah's name is the secret to success. For as Ibn ʿAṭā'allāh al-Iskandarī ؒ states:

لا تَسْتَغْرِبْ وُقُوعَ الأَكْدارِ، مَا دُمْتَ فِي هَذِهِ الدَّارَ، فَإِنَّهَا
مَا أَبْرَزَتْ إِلا مَا هُوَ مُسْتَحِقٌّ وَصْفِهَا وَوَاجِبُ نَعْتِهَا

"So long as you are in this world, be not surprised at the existence of sorrow, for truly it manifests nothing but what is in keeping with its character or its inevitable nature."

The life in this lowly world is transitory, and the way to achieve salvation in the afterlife is by accepting the trials decreed by Allah عز وجل and exercising patience. It is times of difficulty when our character and religiosity is tested at the highest level, and one cannot claim to be a friend of Allah عز وجل and a sincere believer if they cannot overcome the waves of tribulation. The true believer has a long-term outlook and realizes that the happiness and pleasures of this world sometimes must be curbed in order to pave the way for true success in the permanent plane of bliss in the Hereafter.

20

Why is everything falling apart?

Nothing in this life is stable. Times of happiness sometimes become converted into moments of sadness, and good trends become replaced with difficult currents. But there are some critical moments in life where everything seems to fall apart, and not even a semblance of stability remains. At such damaging junctures, a person may become hopeless and feel that even the smallest of their blessings are being taken away from them. Naturally, a person afflicted with such a trial may ask: “Why is Allah ﷻ depriving me of all the means of support and stability that I have? Why can I not be given a little bit of support?”

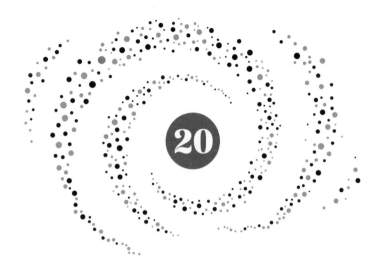

The aforementioned scenario is the exact sequence of events that occurred in the life of the blessed Prophet ﷺ after the Battle of Badr. Fresh from a resounding victory against the polytheists, the Muslims were in a positive mode, as they witnessed first-hand the support of Allah ﷻ in the battlefield through the intervention of the Angels and other miraculous events. After arriving back in Medina, the Muslims sought to celebrate their triumph against the enemies of the truth, with their faith being rejuvenated and strengthened at an unforeseen level. But in the midst of this struggle, the Ummah was struck with a grave tragedy as Ruqayyah رضي الله عنها—the beloved daughter of the Prophet ﷺ—suddenly passed away on the same day of victory. Such a sharp downward shift in life is a reality decreed by Allah ﷻ on His creation, whereby a *ni'mah* (benefaction) is usually followed by an *imtiḥān* (test). Ibn 'Umar رضي الله عنهما relates that the Prophet ﷺ would usually make the following prayer in his lifetime:

اللَّهُمَّ إِنِّي أَعُوذُ بِكَ مِنْ زَوَالِ نِعْمَتِكَ وَتَحَوُّلِ عَافِيَتِكَ وَفُجَاءَةِ نِقْمَتِكَ وَجَمِيعِ سَخَطِكَ

"O Allah, I seek refuge in You from the sudden decline of Your blessings, and the sudden change from being in a state of well-being, and the suddenness of Your vengeance, and from all forms of Your wrath."

Tests are a regular feature of life in this temporal world, but what further compounds the issue is that such tribulations do not occur in a stable fashion; instead, they may come together in the form of a heavy bundle. Owing to the unpredictable nature of such tests, Muslims are encouraged to often seek

Allah's refuge from the sudden removal of blessings and benefactions in one's life. Such dangerous moments can disturb the psyche of even the most stable and practicing Muslim, and thereby plunge them into chaos. The blessed Prophet ﷺ himself was forced to face such a pressing series of tests in a difficult time period that was known as *'Ām al-Ḥuzn* (The Year of Sorrow), during which he was brutally expelled by the people of Ṭā'if, an event which was then followed with the tragic deaths of his wife Khadījah رضي الله عنها and his uncle Abū Ṭālib. To further add to the pain and suffering, the Prophet ﷺ and his small group of followers were subject to a severely stiff boycott. Undoubtedly, *'Ām al-Ḥuzn* was the most difficult stretch of time for the blessed Prophet ﷺ throughout his 23 year mission. Nevertheless, the Prophet ﷺ persevered and he was able to overcome the challenges of that time period, such that he was able to successfully carry the message of Islam to a new frontier and allow it to reach unprecedented success.

During such dark and challenging spells of time in which all our blessings dissolve and disappear in the darkness, a serious moment of introspection and self-evaluation is needed. It may be that this phase was decreed by Allah ﷻ in order to inspire one's repentance or elevate their rank. At first sight, this suggestion may seem absurd or incorrect, since the grateful Muslim's blessings should not go away from them. After all, there is a popular saying in the Muslim ethos which states:

أَلنِعْمَةُ إِذَا شَكَرْتَ قَرَّتْ وَإِذَا كَفَرْتَ فَرَّتْ

"Blessings stay with gratitude and they flee with ingratitude."[115]

So how then can the grateful Muslim have their benefactions and blessings go away? There are two responses to this objection. First and foremost, it is quite likely that their gratitude allowed them to retain some of their blessings—even during their ordeal—which would have otherwise been stripped away from them. Secondly, it is likely that a person's gratitude for their blessings would have caused their prayers to be converted into means of goodness for them on the Day of Judgement. This deferment is a positive sign for the believer, since it means that Allah ﷻ wishes to increase the sum of the yielded benefits in the time period that matters most, namely the Day of Judgement.

In addition, through these losses, Allah ﷻ provides His servant the golden opportunity to accrue rewards through their patience and perseverance.

مَا عِندَكُمْ يَنفَدُ وَمَا عِندَ ٱللَّهِ بَاقٍ وَلَنَجْزِيَنَّ ٱلَّذِينَ صَبَرُوٓا۟ أَجْرَهُم بِأَحْسَنِ مَا كَانُوا۟ يَعْمَلُونَ

"Whatever you have will end, but whatever Allah has is everlasting. And We will certainly reward the steadfast according to the best of their deeds."[116]

---

115 al-Thaʿlabī, *Tamthīl wa al-Muḥāḍarah*, p. 416.

116 *al-Naḥl*, 16:96.

During dark and challenging times in which all our blessings dissolve and disappear, a serious moment of introspection and self-evaluation is needed. It may be that this phase was decreed by Allah ﷻ in order to inspire one's repentance or elevate their rank.

Thus, any loss that the servant sustains this world is not a deficit, but actually a surplus of blessings that will be accrued in this afterlife. This conclusion is also reiterated in the following Quranic verse:

وَلَنَبْلُوَنَّكُم بِشَيْءٍ مِّنَ ٱلْخَوْفِ وَٱلْجُوعِ وَنَقْصٍ مِّنَ ٱلْأَمْوَٰلِ
وَٱلْأَنفُسِ وَٱلثَّمَرَٰتِ ۗ وَبَشِّرِ ٱلصَّٰبِرِينَ

"We will certainly test you with a touch of fear and famine and loss of property, life, and crops. Give good news to those who patiently endure."[117]

This latter verse represents Allah's golden guarantee that any losses that afflict the patient servant will be compensated by even higher gains in the afterlife. This promise from the divine is so strong in its import that Allah ﷻ ordered His Prophet ﷺ to give glad tidings to the ones afflicted in this world: their gains in the afterlife are a matter of certainty. This explains why the Prophet ﷺ once said:

وَمَا أَعْطَى اللَّهُ أَحَدًا مِنْ عَطَاءٍ أَوْسَعَ مِنَ الصَّبْرِ

"And no one is given a better or vaster gift than patience."

The great Imam and Successor al-Ḥasan al-Baṣrī رحمه الله also said:

الصَّبْرُ كَنْزٌ مِن كُنُوزِ الْخَيْرِ

"Patience is a beautiful treasure of good."

---

[117] *al-Baqarah*, 2:155.

Such a fortune is only granted to a believer who is worthy in His majestic sight. In order for a Muslim to qualify for this special rank, they must never be dissatisfied when they are stripped of a blessing, regardless of the amount lost or the exact time that the erasure occurred. The Muslim who loves and trusts his Creator may feel particularly pained by losing a loved one or a cherished thing at a certain point of time, but they should know that Allah ﷻ always knows best. It is possible that if their loved one lived a little bit longer, they may have lost faith or committed an unforgivable wrong. If they stayed longer at a certain post or profession, they may have likely suffered or been exposed to an irreparable harm. This explains why the pious Umayyad-era Caliph ʿUmar ibn ʿAbd al-ʿAzīz ؓ once said: "I have given up on ever trying to overcome the timing of Allah's Decree, and I have sufficed myself with this *duʿā'*:

اللهُمَّ رَضِّنِي بِقَضَائِكَ وَبَارِكْ لِي فِي قَدْرِكَ حَتَّى لَا أُحِبَّ
تَعْجِيلَ شَيْءٍ أَخَّرْتَهُ وَلَا تَأْخِيرَ شَيْءٍ عَجَّلْتَهُ

'O Allah, make me content with Your providence and bless me in Your Decree such that I would not like to hasten what has been delayed nor delay what has been hastened.'"

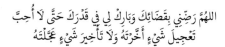

Echoing this sentiment, Ibn ʿAṭāʾallāh al-Iskandarī ﵀ said:

رُبَّمَا وَرَدَتِ الظُّلَمُ عَلَيْكَ لِيُعَرِّفَكَ قَدْرَ مَا مَنَّ بِهِ عَلَيْكَ

"Perhaps He allowed darkness to engulf you so that you could recognize the tremendous blessings He was bestowing upon you."

Many of our life stories in this temporal world will not have happy endings. It is quite possible for our spiritual tests to last for the entire duration of our lives, and the blessings that we aspire to acquire may not be acquired until the Day of Judgement. But the believer has a long-sighted vision that transcends the finite limits of this universe: they know that the afterlife exists with full certainty, and they realize that every loss in this world implies a proportionate gain in the afterlife.

قُل لَّن يُصِيبَنَا إِلَّا مَا كَتَبَ اللَّهُ لَنَا هُوَ مَوْلَانَا وَعَلَى اللَّهِ فَلْيَتَوَكَّلِ الْمُؤْمِنُونَ

Say, "Nothing will ever befall us except what Allah has destined for us. He is our Protector." So in Allah let the believers put their trust.

AL-TAUBAH, 51

21

Is Allah testing or punishing me?

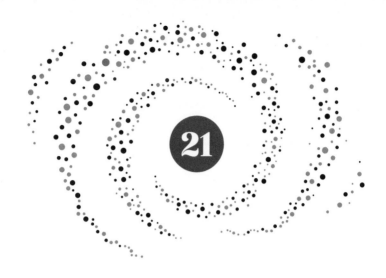

Who had informed you that life in this world would be perfect and fair? Allah ﷻ never promised such a thing to His creation. In actual fact, He explicitly stated in a number of Quranic verses that every person living in this Earth will face trials. Despite this fact, one sometimes is naturally inclined to ask: "Who does Allah test us so much? Is it a punishment? If not, then what is the purpose of such trials?" In this regard, Imam Ibn al-Jawzī ؒ relates the extraordinary story of a man who performed every one of his five prayers in the mosque for more than 80 years. At this point of his life, it so happened that his son passed away. Instead of praying to Allah ﷻ and supplicating to Him on behalf of this son, this man ignorantly said: "There is no point for anyone to make *du'ā'* to Allah because Allah does not listen to anyone's prayers." Ibn al-Jawzī ؒ commented on this shocking account by stating: "I realized that this man was merely worshipping Allah out of habit, but he did not have a relationship based on any knowledge or faith."

Allah ﷻ has condemned this type of mentality by stating:

وَمِنَ النَّاسِ مَنْ يَعْبُدُ اللَّهَ عَلَىٰ حَرْفٍ

"And there are some who worship Allah on the verge [of faith]."[118]

These are the people who worship Allah ﷻ on a slippery stone; their reverence to Him is contingent to whether they receive the blessings that they seek. The moment that Allah ﷻ strips them of a favour or advantage, they immediately abandon their commitment to their faith. This attitude is problematic since it renders one's faith in Allah ﷻ conditional to the retrieval of benefits. Such a person refuses to accept divine tests and ultimately fails to appreciate the importance of such tests. This wrongful attitude can be contrasted with the beautiful supplication that the Prophet ﷺ made to Allah ﷻ after he was shunned by the people of Ṭā'if, where he

118 *al-Ḥajj*, 22:11.

maintained his resolve and said to his Creator:

إِن لَمْ يَكُن بِكَ غَضَبٌ عَلَيَّ فَلَا أُبَالِي

"As long as You are not angry with me, I do not care."

Although it can be difficult to know the exact reason and wisdom behind a divine test, there are some ways to discern a proximate answer. For instance, if the test was preceded by a sin or state of heedlessness, then it is very likely a wake-up call and a chance for one's sins to be erased. But if the test came when one was indulging in the delights of the world and becoming submerged in its comforts, then it is likely that Allah ﷻ wishes to re-awaken His slave from their spiritual slumber. Thirdly, if the test occurred when the servant was performing acts of worship and was engaging in remembrance of Him, then this is likely indicative of His love and His desire to purify His servants and ensure they are perfected.

But the sole way to know if Allah's test is due to His love or punishment is gauging one's response to this divine trial. This point was alluded by the Prophet ﷺ in the following Hadith:

إِذَا أَرَادَ اللَّهُ بِعَبْدِهِ الْخَيْرَ عَجَّلَ لَهُ الْعُقُوبَةَ فِي الدُّنْيَا وَإِذَا أَرَادَ اللَّهُ بِعَبْدِهِ الشَّرَّ أَمْسَكَ عَنْهُ بِذَنْبِهِ حَتَّى يُوَفَّى بِهِ يَوْمَ الْقِيَامَةِ

"When Allah wants good for His slave, He hastens his punishment in this world. And when He wants bad for His slave, He withholds his sins from him until he appears before Him on the Day of Judgment."

Thus, if one faces consequences for their sins in this world, then this is a positive sign, since it indicates that Allah ﷻ wishes to purify them before meeting them in the afterlife. On the other hand, if a person is sinning and they do not face any consequences in this world, then it means that He potentially wishes them to be punished in the afterlife. The Prophet ﷺ beautifully encapsulated this rule by stating:

إِنَّ عِظَمَ الْجَزَاءِ مَعَ عِظَمِ الْبَلاَءِ

"And certainly the greater reward comes with the greater trial."

Thus, the greater the degree that a person is tested, the greater the reward they will accrue. The Prophet ﷺ gave glad tidings to the one who is tested:

وَإِنَّ إِذَا أَحَبَّ قَوْماً اِبْتَلاَهُمْ، فَمَنْ رَضِيَ فَلَه الرِّضَا، وَمَنْ سَخِطَ فَلَه السُّخْطُ

"And indeed when He (Allah) loves a people, He subjects them to tests. Whoever receives divine tests with contentment, they will be blessed with Allah's pleasure. As for the one who reacts with anger and frustration, then they will be exposed to His wrath."[119]

The choice in how one reacts lies squarely in the hands of the servant. Should they respond with contentment and humility instead of anger and arrogance, then Allah ﷻ will elevate

119 *Sunan al-Tirmidhī*, 2396.

their station and rank in the Hereafter. In a beautiful Hadith, the Prophet ﷺ said:

إِذَا أَحَبَّ اللَّهُ عَبْدًا حَمَاهُ الدُّنْيَا كَمَا يَظَلُّ أَحَدُكُمْ يَحْمِي سَقِيمَهُ الْمَاءِ

"If Allah loves His slave, He protects him from this dunyā (temporal world) the way that one of you would hold back water from your loved one when they are sick."

The Prophet ﷺ explained the love of Allah ﷻ for His servants through a beautiful analogy. If a person is sick with a serious illness, there may be circumstances where they are not permitted to drink cold water, even if they may wish to be nourished with it. It may be painful to deny their requests for it, but one must let the prescribed course of treatment to take its course, or otherwise the cause of the illness will be aggravated. That water is not denied to them out of malice or ill-will, but out of pure love. It may be painful for one to say no to them, but such a measure is necessary for preserving their well-being in the long run. Allah ﷻ interacts in the same way with His servants. He loves them and sometimes withholds from them the things that they desire for their own good. The pain and discomfort that the Muslim faces in this world will not go to waste, but instead will be converted into rewards in the Hereafter.

But there is no doubt that the disappointment of the moment leaves a bitter taste in the mouth and incredibly shakes one's disposition. Can there be a solution for such a malady? Perhaps the most important means of thwarting such misgivings is to improve one's mentality and be optimistic that Allah ﷻ will sooner or later provide His aid and relief. Even if the failures continue to pile up, one should be thankful of what they still have and pray for more from His Grace. Ibn 'Awn ؒ said in this regard:

اِرْضَ بِقَضَاءِ اللهِ عَلَى مَا كَانَ مِنْ عُسْرٍ وَيُسْرٍ؛ فَإِنَّ ذَلِكَ أَقَلَّ لِهَمِّكَ، وَأَبْلَغَ فِيمَا تَطْلُبُ مِنْ آخِرَتِكَ، وَاعْلَمْ أَنَّ العَبْدَ لَنْ يُصِيبَ حَقِيقَةَ الرِّضَا حَتَّى يَكُونُ رِضَاهُ عِنْدَ الفَقْرِ وَالبُؤْسِ كَرِضَاهُ عِنْدَ الغِنَاءِ وَالرَّخَاءِ، كَيْفَ تَسْتَقْضِي اللهَ فِي أَمْرِكَ ثُمَّ تَسْخَطُ إِنْ رَأَيْتَ قَضَاءَهُ مُخَالِفًا لِهَوَاكَ؟ وَلَعَلَّ مَا هَوَيْتَ مِنْ ذَلِكَ لَوْ وُفِّقَ لَكَ لَكَانَ فِيهِ هَلَكَتُكَ، وَتَرْضَى قَضَاءَهُ إِذَا وَافَقَ هَوَاكَ؟ وَذَلِكَ لِقِلَّةِ عِلْمِكَ بِالغَيْبِ، وَكَيْفَ تَسْتَقْضِيهِ إِنْ كُنْتَ كَذَلِكَ مَا أَنْصَفتَ مِنْ نَفْسِكَ، وَلَا أَصَبْتَ بَابَ الرِّضَا

"Be content with the Decree of Allah in both times of hardship and ease, for reaching the state of contentment will ease your worries and is better for your Hereafter. The state of contentment cannot be achieved unless if one is satisfied with Allah in all circumstances, whether in times of ease or difficulty. And know that you cannot attain true contentment until you are just as content in a state of poverty or test, as you are in a state of wealth and ease. And how can you request from Allah abundance in your affairs and then get angry if you think His Decree conflicts with your desires? Perhaps the only reason this happens is because of your lack of knowledge of the unseen."

You might not be able to see it, but the tragedies and trials that you go through in this world are currently being converted into rewards in the Hereafter. For instance, if you have lost a baby or young child in this life, you should know that it is currently stationed in a beautiful household of Paradise under the care of the Prophet Ibrāhīm ﷺ, and it awaits your arrival. When your child passed away and you invoked the *ḥamd* (praise) of Allah ﷻ, He built in your name multiple mansions in Paradise. Once you reach your final destination, you will come to the realization that all your efforts and trials were worth the price. The person who lacks this long-term vision becomes ungrateful and falls in the danger of becoming a disbeliever:

فَأَمَّا ٱلْإِنسَٰنُ إِذَا مَا ٱبْتَلَىٰهُ رَبُّهُۥ فَأَكْرَمَهُۥ وَنَعَّمَهُۥ فَيَقُولُ رَبِّىٓ أَكْرَمَنِ
وَأَمَّآ إِذَا مَا ٱبْتَلَىٰهُ فَقَدَرَ عَلَيْهِ رِزْقَهُۥ فَيَقُولُ رَبِّىٓ أَهَٰنَنِ

***"Now, whenever a human being is tested by their Lord through His generosity and blessings, they boast, 'My Lord has honoured me!' But when He tests them by limiting their provision, they protest, 'My Lord has humiliated me!'"*[120]**

Ibn ʿAṭā'allāh al-Iskandarī ﵀ also states:

لِيُخَفِّفْ أَلَمَ البَلاءِ عَلَيْكَ عِلْمُكَ بِأَنَّهُ سُبْحانَهُ هُوَ المُبْلِي لَكَ.
فَالَّذي واجَهَتْكَ مِنْهُ الأَقْدارُ هُوَ الَّذي عَوَّدَكَ حُسْنَ الاخْتِيارِ

"Let the pain of tribulation be lightened for you by knowing that it is the Most Glorious Who is putting you through this trial for the One Who has confronted you with His blows of fate is the same One Who has accustomed you to His choosing well."

120 *al-Fajr,* 89:15-16.

When hardships continuously accumulate in this world and appear unabated, you must always bear in mind that the temporal world is merely a testing ground to gauge your patience and your contentment with Allah's Divine Decree. Moments of ease will come, but one must realize that the life of this world is cyclical in nature, such that moments of comfort and tranquillity are followed by times of difficulty and pestilence. The believer must be able to rise up to their external circumstances and have the capacity to be pleased with Allah's Decree, regardless of whether they are undergoing times of difficulty or ease.

قُل لَّن يُصِيبَنَا إِلَّا
مَا كَتَبَ ٱللَّهُ لَنَا هُوَ مَوْلَىٰنَا
وَعَلَى ٱللَّهِ فَلْيَتَوَكَّلِ ٱلْمُؤْمِنُونَ

Say, "Nothing will ever befall us except what Allah has destined for us. He is our Protector." So in Allah let the believers put their trust.

AL-TAUBAH, 51

22

Can I escape the outcome of my sins?

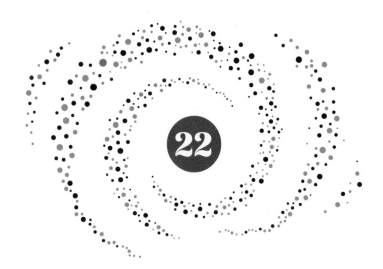

Is it possible to sin too much and go beyond the realm of divine forgiveness? Will a person's sins and faults encircle them throughout their life and haunt them forever? The prospect of one being stuck in the abyss of one's moral crimes and wrongdoings is a perplexing proposition. Although it is always possible for one to be touched with the Grace of the Divine, one must take their past wrongs seriously and ensure that they are regretful of any errors they fell into in their lives. If one reflects on the past stories of the Prophets عليهم السلام, the Companions رضي الله عنهم, and other righteous folk, they will find many moving stories. For example, the father of humanity, Adam 🕊, is reported to have cried for more than 200 years after being expelled from Paradise. Likewise, the Prophet Yūnus 🕊 was at the risk of being dissolved within the bowels of a ferocious leviathan in the depths of the raging sea.

The burden of sin can be difficult to bear. If its underlying roots are left unaddressed, one's destiny and life trajectory can take a turn for the worse in a number of ways. For one thing, a person can be deprived of their *rizq* (provision). Regarding this, the Prophet 🕊 said:

إِنَّ الْعَبْدَ لَيُحْرَمُ الرِّزْقَ بِالذَّنْبِ يُصِيبُه

"Verily a man may be deprived of provision by a sin that he commits."[121]

Sometimes the decline that a person faces in their current day-to-day life routine may be traced to a sin that they committed many years ago but whose effects materialize in the present stage. When Imam Ibn Sīrīn 🕊 found himself in a state of crippling debt, he started to become worried and said:

إِنِّي لَأَعْرِفُ هذَا الْغَمَّ بِذَنْبٍ أَصَبْتُه مُنْذُ أَرْبَعِينَ سَنَةٍ

"It is likely that these worries are a result of a sin that I committed 40 years ago."

---

[121] *Sunan Ibn Mājah*, 4022.

Moreover, sins can affect the vitality and strength of our relationships. One of the pious predecessors used to say:

إِنِّيْ لَأَعْصِيْ اللهَ فَأَرَى ذَالِكَ فِيْ خُلُقِ دَابَتِيْ وَامْرَأَتِيْ

"When I transgress against Allah, I see the consequences of that sin in my riding animal and even in my spouse."

This implies that the commission of sin gradually leads to the breakdown of the basic elements of life. Problems will begin to emerge in the household, one will suffer at their workplace, and their car and other means of transportation will begin to become abysmal—all of these problems will stem from sins, which uproot blessings in one's life. After becoming Caliph, Muʿāwiyah ﵁ received a letter of admonition from ʿĀ'ishah ﵂ which contained the following words:

إِنَّ الْعَبْدَ إِذَا أَمِرَ بِمَعْصِيَةِ اللهِ عَادَ حَامِدُه مِنَ النَّاسِ ذِامّاً

"Verily if a person sins, even those who previously used to praise him will turn against him."

Undoubtedly, there are many circumstances where a person's sins has a negative bearing on their character, which in turn causes them to hurt many other people through their interpersonal interactions. This may lead to a dark and negative cycle of socially deleterious behaviour, whereby one unleashes their anger and frustration at others.

Over time, this type of behaviour creates barriers between a person and their loved ones, with this isolation leading to other sins as well. The believer should exert their best efforts to prevent such a negative state of affairs from transpiring by maintaining their good character. Umm al-Dardā' 🙞 narrates that on one night, she found her husband Abū al-Dardā' 🙞 praying to Allah and continuously making one supplication to Allah: that his character be beautified. She carefully watched him and found that he continued making this supplication until the time of the Fajr prayer arrived. This remarkable course of action caused Umm al-Dardā' 🙞 to ask Abū al-Dardā' 🙞 why he restricted himself to just making that *du'ā'* (supplication). In his response, Abū al-Dardā' 🙞 said: "O Umm al-Dardā', if a person has good character they naturally affect so many people in beautiful ways such that they would make *du'ā'* for that person and he would enter Paradise as a result. Whereas if a person has bad character, they would hurt so many people without even realizing it that they would make *du'ā'* against him and end up leading him to the Hellfire."

But even if one's sins affect other individuals, a path of redemption still does exist such that one will be able to clean their slate of evil deeds. A person can purify and rejuvenate themselves through the path of sincere *tawbah* (repentance), which according to Ibn al-Qayyim 🙞 leads one to a beautiful and exalted station. For as he puts it, when a sinner sincerely repents, it leads to the following state:

كَسْرَةٌ خَاصَّةٌ تَحْصُلُ لِلْقَلْبِ

"...a special type of brokenness that happens in the heart [of the sinner]."[122]

The ability to find Allah ﷻ once more after being in a state of sin creates a special moral faculty in the heart that pleases Him in an unprecedented manner. This point can be appreciated from a Hadith that describes the intense pleasure of Allah ﷻ when His slave repents:

لَلَّهُ أَشَدُّ فَرَحًا بِتَوْبَةِ أَحَدِكُمْ مِنْ أَحَدِكُمْ بِضَالَّتِهِ إِذَا وَجَدَهَا

"Allah is even more joyous with the repentance of His servant when He turns towards Him than one of you would when finding your lost camel with all of your possessions on it."[123]

Imam Ibn al-Qayyim ؒ mentioned that after Adam ؑ was expelled from Paradise, Shayṭān danced with joy and believed that he had attained a resounding victory against him. But he failed to realize that the one who dives into the bottom of the ocean is able to retrieve the most valuable of gems and pearls. Likewise, when Yūnus ؑ sunk to the bottom of the ocean after being swallowed by a whale, Allah ﷻ accepted his repentance and said:

---

122 Ibn al-Qayyim, *Madārij al-Sālikīn*, p. 163.

123 *Ṣaḥīḥ Muslim*, 2747.

فَٱجْتَبَٰهُ رَبُّهُۥ فَجَعَلَهُۥ مِنَ ٱلصَّٰلِحِينَ

"Then his Lord chose him, making him one of the righteous." [124]

At the end, Adam ﷺ emerged victorious. He will re-enter Paradise once more, but this time he will obtain an even higher rank and on this occasion will be accompanied with his progeny. After surviving his terrible ordeal, Yūnus ﷺ returned once more to his people, who had previously rejected him. But this time, they had accepted his call and were to ready to accept the message of monotheism. From these aforementioned facts, Ibn 'Aṭā'allāh al-Iskandarī ﷺ derives the following maxim:

إِذَا وَقَعَ مِنْكَ ذَنْبٌ فَلاَ يَكُنْ سَبَبًا لِيَأْسِكَ مِنْ حُصُولِ الاسْتِقَامَةِ مَعَ رَبِّكَ ، فَقَدْ يَكُونُ ذَلِكَ آخِرَ ذَنْبٍ قُدِّرَ عَلَيْكَ

"When you commit a sin, do not let it be a cause for despair to attain righteousness with your Lord, for that may be the last sin that Allah ever destined for you to commit."

Allah ﷻ is always pleased when His slave turns back to Him, and every episode of repentance raises a person to a higher and unprecedented rank in the sight of their Creator. That way, a person can become the best version of themselves and serve the Ummah in the most productive way possible.

---

124 *al-Qalam*, 68:50.

23

Why is there so much suffering in the world?

Why is it the case that tragedies and disasters occur to morally upright and innocent people? Why is the world currently ablaze with genocides, disasters, and life-threatening diseases? Why are so many innocent people being slaughtered and killed by bloodthirsty people? If Allah ﷻ is all-Loving and all-Merciful, then why do such crimes occur on a daily basis? What can we do in our individual and collective roles to combat such injustices?

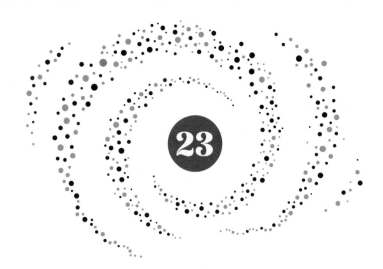

A monumental *du'ā'* (supplication) that the Prophet ﷺ made was the following:

لَبَّيكَ وَسَعْدَيكَ وَالْخَيْرُ كُلُّهُ بِيَدَيكَ وَالشَّرُّ لَيْسَ إِلَيْكَ أَنَا بِكَ وَإِلَيْكَ تَبَارَكْتَ وَتَعَالَيْتَ

"Here I am, O Allah, in answer to Your call, fully pleased to serve You. All good is in Your Hands and evil should never be attributed to You. I exist by Your Will and will return to You. How blessed and exalted are You!"

Imam Ibn al-Qayyim ﷺ commented on this splendid report by stating:

فَتَبَارَكَ وَتَعَالَى عَن نِسْبَةِ الشَّرِّ إِلَيْهِ بَلْ كُلُّ مَا نُسِبَ إِلَيْهِ فَهُوَ خَيْرٌ
وَالشَّرُّ إِنَّمَا صَارَ شَرًّا لِإِنْقِطَاعِ نِسْبَتِهِ وَإِضَافَتِهِ إِلَيْهِ

"Allah is far more glorified and exalted that someone should attribute evil to Him. Rather the only thing attributed to Him is good. And evil only becomes evil because it is removed from what it was originally attributed to, and then wrongly assigned to Him."[125]

In another narration, a man approached the Prophet ﷺ and asked him for sincere and worthy advice. The Prophet ﷺ imparted to him the following words:

لَا تَتَّهِمِ اللّٰهُ فِيْ شَيْءٍ قَضَاهُ لَكَ

"Do not blame Allah for something He decreed for you."

125 Ibn al-Qayyim, *Shifā' al-'Alīl*, p. 178.

The individuals who often assign blame to Allah ﷻ for the problems and maladies that arise in their society become blind-sighted and fail to uphold their own responsibilities as caretakers in this world. Regarding the responsibility of humans for the problems that plague the Earth, Allah ﷻ said:

ظَهَرَ ٱلْفَسَادُ فِي ٱلْبَرِّ وَٱلْبَحْرِ بِمَا كَسَبَتْ أَيْدِي ٱلنَّاسِ لِيُذِيقَهُم
بَعْضَ ٱلَّذِي عَمِلُوا۟ لَعَلَّهُمْ يَرْجِعُونَ

"Corruption has spread on land and sea as a result of what people's hands have done, so that Allah may cause them to taste some of their deeds and perhaps they might return [to the Right Path]."[126]

When Allah ﷻ proclaimed to the assembly of Angels that He was going to create and then locate humankind on Earth so that they may care for it as stewards and caretakers, the Angels said:

أَتَجْعَلُ فِيهَا مَن يُفْسِدُ فِيهَا وَيَسْفِكُ الدِّمَاءَ

"They asked [Allah], 'Will You place in it someone who will spread corruption there and shed blood while we glorify Your praises and proclaim Your holiness?'"[127]

126 *al-Rūm*, 30:41.

127 *al-Baqarah*, 2:30.

Allah made it crystal-clear to the Angels that He knows best what His creation will do on the Earth and how many of them will use their free will to serve Him and His religion.

Allah ﷻ responded to their query by stating:

إِنِّي أَعْلَمُ مَا لَا تَعْلَمُونَ

"I know what you do not know."[128]

Allah made it crystal-clear to the Angels that He knows best what His creation will do on the Earth and how many of them will use their free will to serve Him and His religion. Some exegetes and commentators add that Allah ﷻ was alluding to His knowledge of the many Prophets ﷺ, martyrs, and righteous folk who will live on this Earth and disseminate the pure and untainted teachings of His religion for many generations to come. The existence of so many blessed individuals—with the final Prophet and Messenger ﷺ being at the apex—makes the creation of humankind entirely worthwhile.

But what about all the evil that exists in this world? A person may acknowledge the presence of many righteous individuals and paragons of virtue throughout history, but they will nevertheless contend that the Earth is still full of many trials, tribulations, wars, and injustices. These constant waves of chaos have been designed with the purpose of driving conscious humans to their Creator ﷻ, Who is the source of concord and harmony. The evil in this world is what pushes humans to connect with Allah ﷻ and appreciate the majesty of His names in the world. Had there been no poverty and destitution, one would not be able to appreciate the beauty of Allah's name *al-Karīm* (The Most Generous). If there was no pain and

---

128 *al-Baqarah*, 2:30.

discomposure in this world, one would not be able to connect with the divine names of *al-Ṣabūr* (The Most Patient) and *al-Ḥalīm* (The Forbearing).

Throughout the annals of history, one can find glittering stories and examples of God-conscious folk that should be followed and emulated. For instance, a Companion by the name of Zayd ibn Ṣawḥān had his hand severely injured in a battle, but he was smiling when the blood was flowing. The people passing by him were surprised by this sight and asked him why he was delighted notwithstanding his injury. He said with full confidence: "It is a pain that has come and will be soothed by the reward of Allah. And in my smiling, there is comfort for those believers who will follow my example." Even today, we find this golden example being embodied by people of courage and moral fibre. In Gaza, for instance, there have been countless individuals who have had their entire households and neighbourhoods destroyed, yet they have accepted such trials with a smile. These signs of faith and resilience should awaken others from their state of heedlessness and remind them of the many blessings that they have taken for granted. It is narrated that the Prophet Dāwūd once asked Allah why there is so much suffering in the world. Allah responded that the reason is that He loves for His servants to turn back to Him in gratitude. Sometimes crises and accidents are needed to pull a person away from the mundanity and useless cycles of this life so that they can re-orient themselves towards a bigger purpose that is directed to the divine. Paradoxically, such negative moments in life push one away from sin and cause them to lead a cause that is directed to serving the Ummah. Having an Ummatic vision is what causes one to cease listing their petty grievances and instead focusing on the major challenges that the Muslim world currently faces. Once a Muslim acquires and shares this collective consciousness, they know that they can no longer complain about the personal struggles that they face and instead exercise a pure and beautiful form of altruism vis-à-vis their Muslim brothers and sisters throughout the world.

The fate of every believing soul has already been written by Allah ﷻ, and can be expressed through a general rule that has been expressed in the following prophetic Hadith found in *Ṣaḥīḥ al-Bukhārī*: "No fatigue, nor disease, nor sadness, nor pain, nor distress befalls a Muslim, even if it were the prick he receives from a thorn, except that Allah removes some of his sins for that." The Ummah as a whole has been decreed its collective share of mercy if it patiently overcomes the trials and tribulations of this world. The Prophet ﷺ said:

أُمَّتِي هَذِهِ أُمَّةٌ مَرْحُومَةٌ لَيْسَ عَلَيْهَا عَذَابٌ فِي الْآخِرَةِ
عَذَابُهَا فِي الدُّنْيَا الْفِتَنُ وَالزَّلَازِلُ وَالْقَتْلُ

"This nation of mine is a nation covered in mercy. It has no torment in the Hereafter, but rather its torment is only here in this world, through its tribulations, earthquakes, and killing."

Thus, how one responds to these trials is key and indicative of whether they are following the Muslim paradigm of patience. Instead of asking why Allah ﷻ is sending a particular form of hardship, one should ask how they are responding to it to attain His pleasure. In this regard, Ibn ʿAṭāʾallāh al-Iskandarī ؒ said:

إِذَا أَرَدْتَ أَنْ يَفْتَحَ لَكَ بَابَ الرَّجَاءِ فَاشْهَدْ مَا مِنْهُ إِلَيْكَ ،
وَإِذَا أَرَدْتَ أَنْ يَفْتَحَ لَكَ بَابَ الْخَوْفِ فَاشْهَدْ مَا مِنْكَ إِلَيْهِ

"If you want the door of hope to be opened for you, then consider what comes to you from Him. But if you want the door of fear open for you, then consider what goes to Him from you."

Nothing on this Earth occurs without a divine wisdom, and your current trials and tribulations are no exception to this rule. Your very existence on this planet and every passing moment of your life constitutes an opportunity for you to decipher the purpose of life and re-orient your conduct towards the Divine. Any personal problem that you are facing during your time on this Earth constitutes a purification of your sins and an opportunity for you to give up your individualistic lens and adopt an Ummatic vision instead. Once you are able to understand the divine laws that govern this world and how Allah's Wisdom goes beyond the individual level, you will be able to diagnose your tests through a positive and religiously-coloured perspective.

24

Do good deeds extend my life?

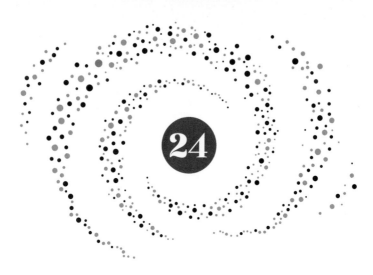

Every person has been destined to be tested in this world, and to also witness the tests of others. But one is not simply required to withstand hardships in this world. Rather, one is also required to help others to the best of their ability. Giving charity has a positive and long-lasting effect on one's decree, and it should be used effectively by Muslims to amplify their register of good deeds in the Afterlife. Perhaps one of the greatest luminaries that can be mentioned in this regard is Zaynab bint Khuzaymah. She was the widow of the Companion ʿAbdullāh ibn Jaḥsh, who was tragically martyred in the Battle of Uḥud. Notwithstanding this horrible event, Zaynab was a woman of deep faith and conviction, and she was known for her love of the poor; she would regularly give *ṣadaqah* (voluntary charity) to the paupers and impoverished people that lived in her locality. The Prophet ﷺ was amazed by her generosity, and he subsequently married her in the fourth year of the Hijrah. But just a few months later, she would shockingly pass away; with the exception of Khadījah ◈, this would make her the only wife of the Prophet ﷺ to pass away during his lifetime and the first to be buried in al-Baqīʿ. This story warrants some reflection. Perhaps the most astounding fact about it is that Allah ◈ decreed for Zaynab to live just long enough to be married by the Prophet ﷺ, which is undoubtedly a great blessing that will continue to benefit her in the Hereafter as well. It is quite likely that it was her good deeds—such as her incredible patience after the death of her first husband and her generosity to the poor—that afforded her this great fortune.

A person's legacy constitutes the culmination of their collective lifetime efforts. This includes every achievement, every problem that was overcome, and every challenge or crisis that was defused. Through these efforts, one will leave a noticeable mark in their society in one way or another, from which the upcoming generations can benefit. For instance, if a person smiled towards a nervous child entering a mosque for the first time, this would likely leave a positive impression for the latter and encourage them to visit more in the future. They may have uttered a word of wisdom to a friend that was going through a crisis that allowed them to overcome their difficulties and improve their life. Or they may have helped a person in a dire state of need, such as a person affected by a car crash, and then impressing them with their manners so much that the aided party considered accepting Islam. These glittering moments do not only shape one's legacy, but they also may positively affect one's destiny. Should a pious figure altruistically help another person and allow them to be saved from a threat or difficulty, Allah ﷻ will return the favour: He will provide them a handsome recompense by increasing their lifespan and provision so that their legacy will be amplified. In sum, if you are benevolent to others, Allah ﷻ will be benevolent with you.

This ultimately means that a person's lifespan and legacy can be elongated and increased from its original parameters. After all, the Prophet ﷺ said: "Nothing extends a person's life like good deeds." But at first sight, this seems to be contrary to the understanding of the following Quranic verse:

فَإِذَا جَاءَ أَجَلُهُمْ لَا يَسْتَأْخِرُونَ سَاعَةً وَلَا يَسْتَقْدِمُونَ

"And when their ajal [lifespan] arrives, they cannot delay it for a moment, nor could they advance it."[129]

The scholars have reconciled between these texts by stating that the *ajal* actually consists of two categories: *ajal muṭlaq* (unlimited lifespan) and *ajal muqayyad* (limited lifespan). The *muṭlaq* is the one that is only known to Allah ﷻ, while the *muqayyad* is known by the Angels. When a person is first

---

129 *al-Naḥl*, 16:61.

conceived in the womb, Allah ﷻ commands an Angel to record a certain lifespan for His servant. But with the passage of time, there are cases where Allah ﷻ wills to increase the lifespan and bounties of His servant; He thus orders the Angel to revise the wealth and time that the person will spend on the Earth. This process of revision continues until Allah ﷻ finally informs the Angel that the servant's time on the Earth has finished and that their soul may be taken.

This ultimately means that a person's good deeds have a myriad of positive effects on their life, even if they may not be observable. During the lifetime of the Prophet ﷺ, there were two brothers; one of them would stay and study with the Prophet ﷺ, while the other would travel and work in order to provide for both of them. The latter eventually became frustrated with this division of labour, and went to the Prophet ﷺ; he complain that he was doing all the outside work while his brother enjoyed the companionship of the Prophet ﷺ. But the Prophet ﷺ corrected this man's claim by stating:

لَعَلَّكَ تُرْزَقُ بِه

"It might be that Allah only provides for you because you provide for him."[130]

130 *Sunan al-Tirmidhī*, 2345.

In a parallel fashion, the *duʿā’* (supplication) of a parent or a pious elder can dramatically improve the dividends of a person. A prime example of this can be found in the case of Anas ibn Mālik ؓ, who was sent by his mother Umm Sulaym ؓ to serve the Prophet ﷺ. She also asked the Prophet ﷺ to make a *duʿā’* for him, who positively responded to her request and said:

اَللّٰهُمَّ أَكْثِرْ مَالَهُ وَوَلَدَهُ وَأَطِلْ عُمُرَهُ وَاغْفِرْ ذَنْبَهُ

"O Allah, make his wealth and children abundant, increase his years on Earth, and forgive his sins."

The Prophet ﷺ knew that Anas ؓ would become a man of unparalleled piety, and that he would use these material and physical benedictions in a way to serve Allah's faith. And indeed, the Messenger of Allah's supplication would materialize: Anas ؓ would live for over 100 years, and would count as being the last major Companion to die in Islamic history. In fact, it is recorded that he had more than 100 grandchildren during his lifetime.
Anas ibn Mālik ؓ would become extremely wealthy, such that it was said that anything that he touched would turn into gold. He used this wealth to serve the cause of Islam and was known for his generosity. Besides this wealth and possessions, Anas ؓ was a scholar of the Islamic faith and was renowned for being a prolific narrator of Hadith, having transmitted more than 2000 Hadiths from the Prophet ﷺ. It was through his meticulous service to the religion that countless moral and spiritual teachings were preserved and passed on until the present day.
But the converse rule is also true: some people sink and decline tremendously due to their sins. As the scholars note, one of the

punishments of falling into sin is the following:

أَنَّهَا تَمْحُو بَرَكَةَ الْعُمُرِ وَ بَرَكَةَ الرِّزْقِ

"It destroys any blessing you have in your years on Earth or in your wealth on Earth."

While it is true that many sinful and oppressive folk have wealth and belongings in this world, their possessions are all devoid of blessings and ultimately any actions that they undertake will not be pleasurable. The sole yardstick of success which makes a life worthwhile is the remembrance of Allah ﷻ. For as Allah ﷻ states:

مَا عِنْدَكُمْ يَنْفَدُ وَمَا عِنْدَ اللّٰهِ بَاقٍ

"Whatever you have will end, but whatever Allah has is everlasting."[131]

In another verse, He states:

وَالْآخِرَةُ خَيْرٌ وَأَبْقَى

"...even though the Hereafter is far better and more lasting."[132]

131 *al-Naḥl,* 16:96.

132 *al-Aʿlā,* 87:17.

While some lives are relatively shorter in their timespan, they are still more blessed than others. With just the *barakah* (blessing) of a few years they were able to perform wonders in this Earth. Umar ibn ʿAbd al-ʿAzīz ﵀ ascended to the echelons of power when he was just 38, with his short reign—and ultimately the rest of his life—only lasting 2 years. Despite this, he was able to fill the Earth with justice and prosperity. Muʿādh ibn Jabal ﵁ died in his 30s, yet he will be crowed as the leader of the scholars on the Day of Judgement. Similarly, Saʿd ibn Muʿādh ﵁ died when he was only 37, but the Throne of Allah ﷻ shook when he passed away.

The righteous person who dies in a young age leaves this world for a wisdom. Allah ﷻ knew what would have happened if they lived longer beyond that point, and it may have been the case that they would have deviated or trekked a wrong path. Their early death is thus better for them to maintain their positive standing in the Hereafter. In fact, there are some youth and young individuals who left such a positive mark in their short timespan in this world that even after their death they inspire their circle of families and friends to do good; because this inspiration to performing the good counts as a *ṣadaqah jāriyah* (continuous charity) for them, it is as if they are still alive and undertaking virtuous acts in the present setting. Such people may no longer be physically present, but good deeds are being registered in their name through their continuous forms of charity and others willing to perform virtuous deeds in their name. The essential point is that Allah ﷻ has elaborately drawn a plan for every one of His servants, with some being granted a higher standing despite their relatively short lives, owing to the superior quality of their deeds. Regarding this important point, Ibn ʿAṭāʾallāh al-Iskandarī ﵀ said:

رُبَّ عُمُرٍ تَسَعَتْ آمَادُهُ وَقَلَّتْ أَمْدَادُهُ وَرُبَّ عُمُرٍ قَلِيلَةٌ آمَادُهُ كَثِيرَةٌ أَمْدَادُهُ

"Many a life is long in years but meagre in fruits, and many a life is short in years but rich in fruit."

Be mindful of this fact, and aim to perform as many righteous acts as you can in this world to leave a positive legacy. There is no guarantee that you will live a long life, so strive to make your inner circle and the world around a better place through piecemeal measures on a daily basis.

قُل لَّن يُصِيبَنَا إِلَّا مَا كَتَبَ اللَّهُ لَنَا هُوَ مَوْلَانَا وَعَلَى اللَّهِ فَلْيَتَوَكَّلِ الْمُؤْمِنُونَ

Say, "Nothing will ever befall us except what Allah has destined for us. He is our Protector." So in Allah let the believers put their trust.

AL-TAUBAH, 51

25

What if it is too late?

You remember your youth like it was yesterday. Today, however, you can see the signs of aging in every part of your body. Your hair has started to grey, your body is plagued with fatigue, and your joints begin to hurt. You soon come to the realization that time is rapidly progressing, and that life is far more short than was initially expected.

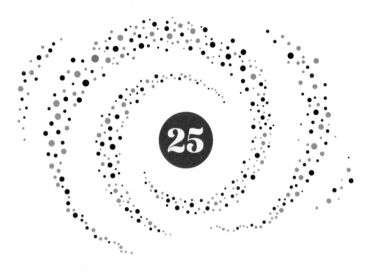

If over time you have decreased your sins and increased your good deeds in your day-to-day activities, then you have aged beautifully, ethically, and gracefully. After all, having an ethical and Islamically conscious view is what orients one to the *ākhirah* (afterlife). The mindful Muslim who analyses the signs of aging on their hair and body realizes that the clock is ticking and prepares for their meeting with their Lord in the other world. This crucial point is illustrated in the following Quranic verse:

أَوَلَمْ نُعَمِّرْكُم مَّا يَتَذَكَّرُ فِيهِ مَن تَذَكَّرَ وَجَاءَكُمُ النَّذِيرُ

"Did We not give you lives long enough so that whoever wanted to be mindful could have done so? And the warner came to you."[133]

Some Quranic exegetes and commentators note that the warner alluded to in this verse does not refer to a Prophet, but a person's grey hairs, which remind a person of their demise. At the same time, scholars note that grey hairs do have many positive elements embedded in them as well. For one thing, they state that having grey hairs is a blessing since it increases a person's dignity, causes them to assume a humble nature, extinguishes their arrogance, and even weakens their desire for this world. The great scholar Imam Ibn Qutaybah ﵀ said:

لَقَدْ جَلَّ قَدرُ الشَّيْبِ إِنْ كَانَ كُلَّمَا بَدَتْ شَيْبَةٌ يَعْرَى مِنَ اللَّهْوِ مَرْكَبُهُ

"The appearance of grey hairs is a great attainment, for its commencement marks the end of vain entertainment."[134]

133 *Fāṭir*, 35:37.

134 Ibn Qutaybah, *'Uyūn al-Akhbār*, vol. 4, p. 53.

One must be cognizant of the rapid pace of this temporal world and aim to live a righteous life, leave a positive mark, and impart the teachings of the religion effectively so that the next generations may benefit.

The blessings accrued from such signs of aging will be primarily deposited in the next world. The Prophet ﷺ is reported to have said:

مَنْ شَابَ شَيْبَةً فِي سَبِيلِ اللَّهِ كَانَتْ لَهُ نُورًا يَوْمَ الْقِيَامَةِ

"Whoever has grown a grey hair in the way of Allah, it will be a light for him on the Day of Judgment."[135]

A person who is given a long life in this world is blessed if they spend their time therein doing good, but it is cursed if they squander their granted period to perform acts of evil. On one occasion, the Prophet ﷺ was asked:

يَا رَسُولَ اللَّهِ أَيُّ النَّاسِ خَيْرٌ

"O Messenger of Allah, who are the best of people?"

The Prophet ﷺ responded by stating:

مَنْ طَالَ عُمُرُهُ وَحَسُنَ عَمَلُه

"Whoever has a long life but uses that long life to do good deeds."

135 *Sunan al-Tirmidhī,* 1635.

He was then asked: "And who are the worst of people?" The Prophet ﷺ said:

مَن طَالَ عُمُرُهُ وَسَاءَ عَمَلُه

"Whoever lives a long life but only increases in sin with that long life."[136]

A person's value is not determined by how long they live, but the deeds that they perform with the time that they are allotted. Regardless of whether someone lives 30 years or 100 years, the time that they spend in this world will feel like the blink of an eye, and it will be over before one even realizes it. By the time one reaches the end of their life, the only thing that will remain is the fleeting memories of the bygone years that passed in quick succession. One must be cognizant of the rapid pace of this temporal world and aim to live a righteous life, leave a positive mark, and impart the teachings of the religion effectively so that the next generations may benefit. In a beautiful Hadith, the Prophet ﷺ said: "No one has more noble of a lineage than Yūsuf. For he is a Prophet, who is the son of a Prophet, who is the son of a Prophet, who is the son of a Prophet." There could not be a more beautiful family line than this: Yūsuf, the son of Ya'qūb, the son of Isḥāq, the son of Ibrāhīm عليهم السلام. In this beautiful chain of prophethood every succeeding generation learnt and absorbed the lessons of their past patriarchs and ensured that no teachings were left behind.

136 *Sunan al-Tirmidhī*, 2330.

It is possible that one has squandered part of their life by engaging in frivolous or valueless activities. While one may be regretful of not capitalizing effectively in their past life, they should not dwell on the negative. It is never too late to make a new start in one's life. In fact, some of the greatest scholars and luminaries of this faith only began their journey of knowledge when their grey hairs had already appeared. For instance, it is narrated that Imam Ibn Ḥazm ﵀ began his journey of knowledge while in his 40s. Likewise, Ṣāliḥ ibn Kaysān ﵀, who was one of the greatest scholars from among the Successors (*Tābi'ūn*), started seeking knowledge at an extremely old age. Regarding him, the great chronicler al-Dhahabī ﵀ said:

إِبْتَدَأَ بِالْعِلْمِ وَهُوَ اِبْنُ سَبْعِيْنَ سَنَةٍ

"He started his journey of knowledge when he was 70 years young."

We should be inspired by these great stories and exert our greatest efforts—regardless of what our age may be—to seek the contentment of Allah ﷻ and attain the best prize in the Hereafter. For just as keeping our bodies healthy and sound is important, it is likewise imperative for one to keep their heart and soul pure.

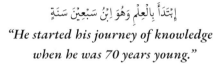

Before one knows it, they will reach the age of 60, which is an extremely important milestone of life and signals that one's life is nearing its end. In an important Hadith, the Prophet ﷺ said that the average lifespan of this Ummah fluctuates between the ages of 60 and 70.[137] In yet another narration, the Prophet ﷺ is reported to have said that Allah ﷻ will continue to forgive a person until they reach the age of 60.[138] This does not necessarily mean that Allah ﷻ will not forgive a person who sins past this age and repents, but instead it is alluding to the fact that a person who persists upon an evil path past the age of 60 is devoid of excuses, and they are jeopardizing their fate on the Day of Resurrection. Another important fact that relates to the later years of life is that they are plagued with hardships and difficulties which can cause one's faith to waver. As such, the Prophet ﷺ would frequently make the following supplication:

أَللَّهُمَّ إِنِّي أَعُوذُ بِكَ مِنَ الْبُخْلِ، وَأَعُوذُ بِكَ مِنَ الْجُبْنِ، وَأَعُوذُ بِكَ أَنْ أُرَدَّ إِلَى أَرْذَلِ الْعُمُرِ، وَأَعُوذُ بِكَ مِنْ فِتْنَةِ الدُّنْيَا وَأَعُوذُ بِكَ مِنْ عَذَابِ الْقَبْرِ

"O Allah, I seek refuge in You from stinginess, and I seek Your protection from cowardice, and I seek Your protection from being returned to feeble old age. And I seek Your protection from the trials of this world and from the torment of the grave."[139]

---

137 *Sunan al-Tirmidhī*, 2331.

138 *Ṣaḥīḥ al-Bukhārī*, 6419.

139 *Sunan al-Nasā'ī*, 5445.

What is noteworthy with this supplication is that the Prophet ﷺ linked seeking refuge from old age with sins and the trials of the Hereafter. This may be an allusion to the intuitive fact that if a person remains a sinner until they become old, they are unlikely to break from their destructive habits. The sooner that one repents and turns back to Allah ﷻ, the more likely that they will be able to cross the finish line of life with a God-conscious smile. Ibn ʿAṭāʾallāh al-Iskandarī ﵀ said:

مِنْ عَلَامَاتِ النَّجَاحِ فِيْ النِّهَايَاتِ اَلرَّجُوْعُ إِلَيْه فِيْ البِدَايَاتِ

"Amongst the signs of success at the end is the turning to Allah in the beginning."

Waiting until the end to repent is a major mistake, as there are no guarantees that one will live a relatively long life. One can and must take the initiative to repent today to have a purer and more religiously oriented tomorrow. The person who takes all necessary precautions and prepares for the Hereafter well in advance will always be pleased and content, while the individual who waits until the very last minute is likely to face Allah ﷻ in the Hereafter short-handed.

26

How can I accept that I am dying?

If you were informed by a trusted source when you would exactly die, what would your reaction be? Would you be alarmed, angry, stressed, or fearful? Regardless of what your answer may be, the fact is that reminders of your own death appear consistently throughout your life, such as when your loved ones, friends, and family members pass away. You yourself may have gone through near-death experiences that remind you of your mortality, and your greying hair provides an explicit message that your days are numbered. The world around you is full of signs of life and death which symbolize the fact that everything in this world is fleeting.

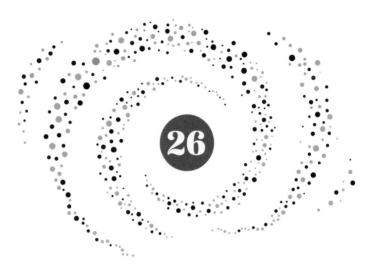

This reality has been expressly articulated in the following Quranic verse:

وَكَأَيِّن مِّنْ ءَايَةٍ فِى ٱلسَّمَٰوَٰتِ وَٱلْأَرْضِ يَمُرُّونَ عَلَيْهَا وَهُمْ عَنْهَا مُعْرِضُونَ

"How many signs in the heavens and the earth do they pass by with indifference!"[140]

This world is a race against time in which one must try to overcome the tribulations of this world and perform as many good deeds as possible. Everyone has a terminal illness already, which is called life; everyone who is born here is also guaranteed to die. But perhaps one of the worst of afflictions is being beset with a sudden death, whereby one is unable to live by their fullest potential. In one important narration, the Prophet ﷺ said:

بَادِروا بِالأَعْمَالِ سَبْعًا هَلْ تَنتَظِرُون إِلَّا فقرًا مُنْسِيًا، أَو غِنًى مُطْغيًا، أَو مَرضًا مُفْسِدًا، أَو هَرَمًا مُفْنِدًا، أَو مَوتًا مُجْهِزًا، أَو الدَّجَّالَ فشَرُّ غَائِبٍ يُنْتظر، أَو السَّاعَةَ فَالسَّاعَةُ أَدْهَى وَأَمَرُّ

"Hasten to do good deeds before you are overtaken by one of seven trials: poverty which causes you to forget your worship, prosperity which corrupts you, a disease that disables you, becoming senile in a way that renders you mentally incapable, sudden death, the Dajjāl, and the Hour, and how tragic and bitter is the Hour!"

140 *Yūsuf*, 12:105.

Receiving the news of a poor prognosis through a divine sign or a trustworthy medical report is a gift from Allah ﷻ, as it provides one the opportunity to make amends with one's family or any other loved ones and to formally say good-bye. Even more importantly, it provides everyone the chance to reflect on their mortality and turn to Allah ﷻ in repentance. Through this divine window a person is given the golden opportunity to properly thank his Creator and engage in His remembrance. Moreover, a person can use any of this spare time in their disposal to undertake good deeds and ask Allah's Forgiveness for sins they have not repented from yet. Despite their fallible status as humans, Allah ﷻ has given each and every one of us chances to reflect on our past lapses and call upon Him in repentance. Despite us falling into sin time and time again, Allah ﷻ is merciful to us and showers us with His blessings, for, as He says:

فَسَبِّحۡ بِحَمۡدِ رَبِّكَ وَٱسۡتَغۡفِرۡهُ

"Then glorify the praises of your Lord and seek His Forgiveness."[141]

This verse constituted the very last imperative that Allah ﷻ issued to the Prophet ﷺ after he led a life of pure goodness. The believer should take heed from this fact and ensure that they inspect their soul for any defects and sins that are in need of rectification. Abū Bakr al-Ṣiddīq ﷺ reported that when death comes to a man, an Angel is told: "Inspect his head."

---

141 *al-Naṣr*, 110:3.

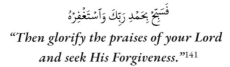

The Angel will then say:

أَجِدُ فِيْ رَأْسِهِ الْقُرْآنُ

"I find the Qur'an in his head."

Then the Angel is asked to analyse his heart, and after his inspection he will report as follows:

أَجِدُ فِيْ قَلْبِهِ الصِّيَامُ

"I find in his heart fasting."

Then the Angel is told to inspect his feet, and after looking at this area, he says:

أَجِدُ فِي قَدَمَيْهِ الْقِيَامِ

"I find in his feet standing in the form of the qiyām (special night) prayer."

It will then be announced by a caller:

حَفِظَ نَفْسَهُ فَحَفِظَهُ اللَّهُ

"This man protected himself, so surely Allah will protect him."

Even when one is deprived of blessings, they should nevertheless be grateful for whatever goodness that remains in their life. Khalīfah ibn Ismā'īl ﵀ relates a fascinating account of a man who was afflicted with leprosy, which ultimately impaired virtually every limb of his body. Despite being seriously disabled by this ailment, Khalīfah ibn Ismāʿīl ﷺ narrated that this man still said: "By your glory, O Allah, if poisonous insects had taken hold of my body and You shredded me to pieces like torn threads, I would only increase—by Your permission—in patience and I would only hold by Your Mercy to nothing but contentment."

But what about if one passes away and they happen to leave dependants? Who will take care of them? There is a beautiful story which illustrates how the believer should orient themselves when they are nearing death and they have family members and children who depend on them. When ʿUmar ibn ʿAbd al-ʿAzīz ﷺ was nearing the end of his life, he had 11 children under his care. His wealth was so little that every child would only inherit 19 dirhams, which was a paltry sum. This immensely worried one of his advisors, who said to the Caliph: "O leader of the believers! We must do something for your children."

إِمَّا أَنْ يَكُونُوا صَالِحِينَ فَاللهُ يَتَوَلَّى الصَّالِحِينَ، وَإِمَّا أَنْ يَكُونُوا غَيْرَ صَالِحِينَ
فَوَاللهِ لَا أَدَعُ لَهُمْ شَيْئًا يَسْتَعِينُونَ بِهِ عَلَى مَعْصِيَةِ اللهِ ﷺ

"If they are righteous, then Allah takes care of the righteous. And if they are not from the righteous, then I do not wish to give them what they will then use to disobey Allah with."

The world around you is full of signs of life and death which symbolize the fact that everything in this world is fleeting. This world is a race against time in which one must try to overcome the tribulations of this world and perform as many good deeds as possible.

In a beautiful passage in his work on aphorisms, Ibn ʿAṭāʾallāh al-Iskandarī ﷺ said:

كَيْفَ يُشْرِقُ قَلْبٌ صُوَرُ الأَكْوَانِ مُنْطَبِعَةٌ فِي مِرْآتِهِ؟ أَمْ كَيْفَ يَرْحَلُ إِلَى اللهِ وَهُوَ مُكَبَّلٌ بِشَهَوَاتِهِ؟ أَمْ كَيْفَ يَطْمَعُ أَنْ يَدْخُلَ حَضْرَةَ اللهِ وَهُوَ لَمْ يَتَطَهَّرْ مِنْ جَنَابَةِ غَفَلاَتِهِ؟ أَمْ كَيْفَ يَرْجُو أَنْ يَفْهَمَ دَقَائِقَ الأَسْرَارِ وَهُوَ لَمْ يَتُبْ مِنْ هَفَوَاتِهِ؟

"How can the heart be illuminated while the mere forms of creatures are reflected in its mirror? How can it journey to Allah while it is shackled by its passions? How can it desire to enter the presence of Allah while it has not yet purified itself of the stain of forgetfulness? How can it understand the subtle secrets in front of it while it has not yet repented of its obvious offences?"

When Allah ﷻ sent Adam ﷺ to the Earth, He said to him:

فَمَن تَبِعَ هُدَايَ فَلَا خَوْفٌ عَلَيْهِمْ وَلَا هُمْ يَحْزَنُونَ

"Then when guidance comes to you from Me, whoever follows it, there will be no fear for them, nor will they grieve."[142]

Similarly, when the Angels take the soul of the righteous person from this Earth:

أَلَّا تَخَافُوا وَلَا تَحْزَنُوا

"Do not fear, nor grieve."[143]

---

142 *al-Baqarah*, 2:38.

143 *Fuṣṣilat*, 41:30.

The Quranic commentators and exegetes states that the phrase "Do not fear" means that the dying believer should not be afraid of what is to come in the Afterlife, while the point "not grieve" means that the person departing from this Earth should not lament those that they are leaving behind. This verse provides relief for the Muslim who is trustful of their Lord, since they gain confidence that their early departure from this world will not lead to any hardship or pain for their loved ones.

قُل لَّن يُصِيبَنَا إِلَّا
مَا كَتَبَ ٱللَّهُ لَنَا هُوَ مَوْلَىٰنَا
وَعَلَى ٱللَّهِ فَلْيَتَوَكَّلِ ٱلْمُؤْمِنُونَ

Say, "Nothing will ever befall us except what Allah has destined for us. He is our Protector." So in Allah let the believers put their trust.

AL-TAUBAH, 51

27

Will Allah still forgive me?

When a person nears the end of their life and only a short interval exists between their stay on this Earth and the transition to the afterlife, they become more conscious and aware of all their wrongs on this Earth. Every crime and sin that they committed flashes back in their mind and confronts them in a sequential manner. This is from Allah's Mercy, as it causes a person to confront their past and purify as many wrongs as possible so that they meet their Creator with a heart that is cleansed. To further dissolve the sins of a person near the end of their life, Allah ﷻ may decree for them to undergo an illness or medical problem, such that their pain expiates their sins and replaces them with virtues in their scroll of deeds.

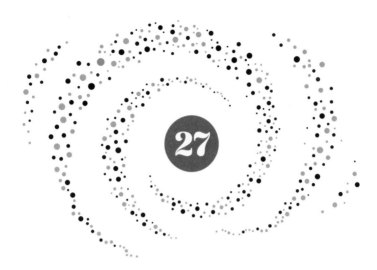

During such moments of fear, pain, and uncertainty, what should our reaction and code of conduct be? The scholars of the Islamic tradition have discussed this topic in relative length, with the most famous one being the analogy of the bird. Ibn Qayyim al-Jawziyyah ﵀ writes that the believer has two wings: the wing of hope and the wing of fear. Ibn al-Qayyim ﵀ argues that throughout a believer's life, there should be a higher degree of fear than hope in a Muslim's disposition, such that they are able to hold their soul accountable to a stronger degree and with urgency rather than simply deferring to Allah's Mercy. But in his adaptation of this analogy, Imam Ibn Kathīr ﵀ notes that when a person nears the point of death, the wing of hope should be assigned preponderance over the wing of fear, since at this point a person's ability to perform deeds is compromised and they should be optimistic of Allah's Grace. While they are fading away in their ever-growing weak state, a person's ability to perform conventional deeds is virtually non-existent. But they should not despair of Allah's Mercy and seek repentance for any lapses and sins that come to their memory during this fragile state.

When a person is on their deathbed or in the fragile state that precedes it, Shayṭān will exert his best efforts to make one heedless of the Mercy of Allah and leave this world in a state of sin. It is reported that when Imam Aḥmad ibn Ḥanbal ﵀ was on the verge of passing away, he kept saying:

لَا لَيْسَ بَعْد

"No, not yet."

His son was surprised to see his father utter such words while he was experiencing the pangs the death, and ultimately asked for clarification. Imam Aḥmad ﷺ said: "I saw Shayṭān in a dream and he was looking defeated. And he said to me, 'O Aḥmad, you have evaded me. I have never been able to take you down.'" But Imam Aḥmad ﷺ would tell him, "No, not yet", in an indication that the battle with the accursed Devil lasts until the very last moment that one is alive on this Earth. Even when one is at their last breaths, Shayṭān tries his very best to make one lose hope of the Mercy of their Creator. During those pressing moments, one should try to remember the Hadith which states that Shayṭān tried to challenge Allah ﷻ, whereby he said:

وَعِزَّتِكَ يَا رَبِّ لَا أَبْرَحُ أُغْوِي عِبَادَكَ مَا دَامَتْ أَرْوَاحُهُمْ فِي أَجْسَادِهِمْ

"By Your glory, O Lord, I will not stop tempting Your slaves so long as their souls are in their bodies."

But Allah responded to him by stating:

وَعِزَّتِي وَجَلَالِي لَا أَزَالُ أَغْفِرُ لَهُمْ مَا اسْتَغْفَرُونِي

"By My Glory and Majesty, I will continue to forgive them so long as they ask Me for forgiveness."[144]

A Muslim should know that lacking any hope in Allah's Mercy is impermissible, especially when one is at their deathbed.

---

144 *Musnad Imām Aḥmad*, 10974.

In one beautiful Quranic verse, Allah ﷻ states:

قُلْ يَٰعِبَادِيَ ٱلَّذِينَ أَسْرَفُوا۟ عَلَىٰٓ أَنفُسِهِمْ لَا تَقْنَطُوا۟ مِن رَّحْمَةِ ٱللَّهِ

"Say [O Prophet, that Allah says]: 'O My servants who have exceeded the limits against their souls! Do not lose hope in Allah's Mercy.'"[145]

Jābir ibn 'Abdullāh ﷺ narrated that he heard the Prophet ﷺ say three days before he died:

لاَ يَمُوتَنَّ أَحَدُكُمْ إِلاَّ وَهُوَ يُحْسِنُ الظَّنَّ بِاللَّهِ

"Let not one of you die except with a good opinion of Allah."

Just before passing away, Abū 'Abd al-Raḥmān al-Sulamī ﷺ is reported to have said:

كَيْفَ لاَ أَرْجُوْ رَبِّيْ وَقَدْ صُمْتُ ثَمَانِيْنَ رَمَضَان

"How could I not have hope in my Lord when I have fasted for Him 80 Ramadans?"

Through these statements, the pious predecessors were not considering their deeds to be sufficient or morally worthy for their salvation. Instead, they were so optimistic of Allah's Mercy that they were certain that even their deficient deeds would be accepted by Him and deemed worthy for them to be

145 *al-Zumar*, 39:53.

granted a reception in Paradise. On one occasion, the Prophet ﷺ met a man who was constantly crying out:

وَا ذُنُوبَاه وَا ذُنُوبَاه

"O my sins, O my sins!"

But the Prophet ﷺ said to him: "Instead of saying, 'O my sins, O my sins,' say,

أَللَّهُمَّ مَغْفِرَتُكَ أَوْسَعُ مِنْ ذُنُوبِي وَرَحْمَتُكَ أَرْجَى عِنْدِي مِنْ عَمَلِي

'O Allah, Your Forgiveness is vaster than my sins and Your Mercy is far more hopeful to me than my deeds.'"

The man read this supplication, but then the Prophet ﷺ ordered him to repeat it again. He was then told to read it once more. After this process was repeated a few times, the Prophet ﷺ said to this man:

قُمْ فَقَدْ غَفَرَ اللّهُ لَكَ

"You may go now, for Allah has forgiven you."

The Mercy of Allah ﷻ is unrestricted and is a sea without any shore. It was this very reality which stunned many of the Companions ﷢ and had them at awe. For instance, when Mu'ādh ibn Jabal ﷺ heard the Prophet ﷺ state that anyone who utters the *shahādah* (testimony of faith) of *lā ilāha illal Allāh* (there is no god but Allah) will enter Paradise, he was pleasantly surprised by this news and said to the Prophet ﷺ: "Should I not go and tell the people?" The Prophet ﷺ

responded by stating: "O Mu'ādh, let the people act." But at the end of one's life, one should say the *shahādah* frequently since at this point one may not be able to perform any other righteous act. All it takes for one to be forgiven unrestrictedly is to utter this great proclamation once with a sincere heart. The Mercy of Allah ﷻ is so boundless that when Fir'awn was on the verge of drowning and frantically sought to proclaim his belief in Allah ﷻ, the Angel Jibrīl ﵇ placed sand in his mouth to prevent him from speaking, lest Allah ﷻ accept his repentance. From this story, one derives the finding that the only conditions needed for attaining Allah's Forgiveness are a sorry heart and a moist tongue.

One does not enter Paradise by virtue of their deeds alone; instead, it is always Allah's Mercy which elevates the value of one's deeds and facilitates their entrance into the permanent garden of bliss. Allah ﷻ loves forgiving so much that He preferred humans to be imperfect sinners rather than perfect and infallible angel-like beings. The Prophet ﷺ said: "If you were not to commit sins, Allah would have swept you out of existence and replaced you with another people who would sin and then seek Allah's Forgiveness and then Allah would forgive them."

This is why Muslims frequently recite the following supplication at the end of every Ramadan:

اللَّهُمَّ إِنَّكَ عَفُوٌّ تُحِبُّ الْعَفْوَ فَاعْفُ عَنِّي

"O Allah, You are the one Who forgives and pardons. You love to forgive, so forgive me."

Just like how the Muslim is hopeful of Allah's Mercy at the end of Ramadan, they can and should be optimistic of His clemency at the final points of their life. Anas ibn Mālik ﷺ reports that the Prophet ﷺ once entered the house of a young man who was dying. The Prophet ﷺ asked him:

كَيْفَ تَجِدُكَ

"How are you feeling?"

The young man responded by saying:

يَا رَسُوْلَ اللّٰهِ أَرْجُوْ اللّٰهَ وَأَخَافُ ذُنُوْبِيْ

"O Messenger of Allah, I have hope in Allah but I fear for my sins."

The Prophet ﷺ said to him: "Then receive the message of glad tidings. For these two feelings are never combined in the heart of a servant in this situation except that Allah will give him what he hopes for and save him from what he fears."
In his famous book on religious maxims and aphorisms, Ibn ʿAṭā'allāh al-Iskandarī ﷺ said:

لَا يَعْظُمُ الذَنْبُ عِنْدَكَ عَظَمَةً تَصُدُّكَ عَنْ حُسْنِ الظَّنِّ بِاللّٰهِ تَعَالَى،
فَإِنَّ مَنْ عَرَفَ رَبَّهُ إِسْتَصْغَرَ فِي جَنْبِ كَرَمِهِ ذَنْبَهُ.

"Let no sin reach such proportions in your eyes that it cuts you off from having a good opinion of Allah. For whoever knows his Lord considers his sins so insignificant when compared to His generosity."

Be optimistic of what you have done for Allah ﷻ and leave the rest to Him. If you are hopeful of meeting Him and believe that He is fair, then He will never turn you down. Have a sincere heart, exert your best efforts to uphold the teachings of Allah's religion and serve the people around you and your sins and lapses will all likely be forgiven on the Day of Judgement.

قُل لَّن يُصِيبَنَآ إِلَّا

مَا كَتَبَ ٱللَّهُ لَنَا هُوَ مَوْلَىٰنَا

وَعَلَى ٱللَّهِ فَلْيَتَوَكَّلِ ٱلْمُؤْمِنُونَ

Say, "Nothing will ever befall us except what Allah has destined for us. He is our Protector." So in Allah let the believers put their trust.

AL-TAUBAH, 51

28

What will the day of my death be like?

The day of a person's death is written by an Angel before they are even born. When that appointed time period comes, the Angel of Death will appear to take their soul. While a person has no choice on the circumstances and the household that receives them at the point of birth, the circumstances revolving around how the Angel of Death will take their soul is entirely predicated on the deeds they perform and the moral choices they made in this world.

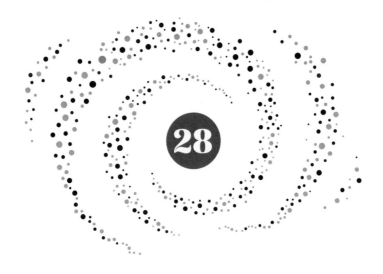

The day of one's death constitutes a pivotal interval period whereby a person is caught between two realms. Throughout history, many of the righteous believers sensed a feeling of their imminent death, with some of them seeing striking dreams that signalled to them that their transition to the other world was near. Perhaps the most dramatic case of this can be found in the story of ʿUthmān ibn ʿAffān ﷺ. In the last night of his life, he went to sleep with the intention of fasting the next day. In a vivid dream that night, he saw the Prophet ﷺ, Abū Bakr, and ʿUmar ﷺ sitting together in a gathering. The Prophet ﷺ gave ʿUthmān ﷺ glad tidings by saying to him, "You will break your fast with us tomorrow, O ʿUthmān." In a parallel fashion, ʿAbdullāh ibn ʿAmr ibn Ḥarām ﷺ, the father of Jābir ibn ʿAbdullāh ﷺ, woke up on the day of the Battle of Uḥud and said to his son, "O Jābir, I have a feeling that I am going to die today. And in fact, I feel that I am going to be the first one to be killed in Uḥud." And just as he foreshadowed it, it so happened that ʿAbdullāh ibn ʿAmr ibn Ḥarām ﷺ was the first martyr of the Battle of Uḥud. Even in modern times, such premonitions recur at an astounding pace. Months before the 2023–2024 Gaza genocide started, thousands of Palestinians witnessed vivid dreams of them and their family members being martyred at the hands of the oppressors.

Scholars argue that the believers are equipped with a special intuition that allows them to anticipate a particular event.

One transmitted report—which has some weakness—states in this regard:

اتَّقُوْا فِرَاسَةَ الْمُؤْمِنِ فَإِنَّهُ يَنْظُرُ بِنُورِ اللَّهِ

"Beware of the believer's intuition, for he sees with the light of Allah."[146]

Even if it were the case that the believer does not have such premonitions, Allah ﷻ facilitates for His close friends the means for a proper ending. Astonishingly, one can find many cases where Muslims have the ability to pray, read the Qur'an, settle their debts, and give charity in their last days. In one beautiful Hadith, the Prophet ﷺ said:

إِذَا أَرَادَ اللَّهُ بِعَبْدٍ خَيْرًا اسْتَعْمَلَهُ

"When Allah wills good for His slave, He uses him."

The Companions رضي الله عنهم then asked the Messenger of Allah :

كَيْفَ يَسْتَعْمِلُهُ

"How does Allah use him?"

The Prophet ﷺ then said:

يُوَفِّقُهُ لِعَمَلٍ صَالِحٍ قَبْلَ الْمَوْتِ

"He gives him the ability to do a good deed right before he dies."

---

146 *Sunan al-Tirmidhī*, 3127.

In yet another report, the Prophet ﷺ said:

إِذَا أَرَادَ اللَّهُ عَزَّ وَجَلَّ بِعَبْدٍ خَيْرًا عَسَلَهُ

"When Allah wills good for His slave, He sweetens him."

The Companions ﷺ then asked: "O Messenger of Allah, how does Allah sweeten His slave?" He said in response:

يَفْتَحُ اللَّهُ عَزَّ وَجَلَّ لَهُ عَمَلًا صَالِحًا قَبْلَ مَوْتِهِ ثُمَّ يَقْبِضُهُ عَلَيْهِ

"Allah guides him to do a righteous deed right before he dies and then He takes his soul while he is in that state."

In an authentic Hadith, the Prophet ﷺ said: "Whoever says *lā ilāha illa Allāh* (there is no god but Allah) seeking Allah's pleasure and this being the last of his deeds will enter Paradise. And whoever gives charity with this being the last of his deeds will enter Paradise."

There are a number of beautiful stories which illustrate the wonderful state in which the pious left this world. Perhaps one of the most notable accounts can be found when ʿUmar ibn ʿAbd al-ʿAzīz ﷺ was on his deathbed. Shortly before he departed from this world, the pious Umayyad Caliph asked his wife Fāṭimah ﷺ to come before him.

The Prophet ﷺ said: "Whoever says lā ilāha illa Allāh (there is no god but Allah) seeking Allah's pleasure and this being the last of his deeds will enter Paradise. And whoever gives charity with this being the last of his deeds will enter Paradise."

Fāṭimah ﵂ obliged and then embraced her husband, who then recited to her the following verse:

إِنَّمَا يُوَفَّى الصَّابِرُونَ أَجْرَهُمْ بِغَيْرِ حِسَابٍ

"Only those who endure patiently will be given their reward without limit." [147]

After some time, 'Umar ibn 'Abd al-'Azīz ﵀ asked his family to leave him alone. His wife and his children respected his wishes, and left the room. But they continued to privately survey him through a small crack in the door. They mentioned that shortly after their departure, a brilliant light shone through the room, causing 'Umar's face to glimmer. After witnessing this spectacle, 'Umar ﵀ said:

مَرْحَباً بِهٰذِهِ الوُجُوْهُ لَيَسَتْ بِوُجُوْهِ إِنْسَانٍ وَلَا جِنّ

"Welcome to these beautiful faces which do not belong to human beings nor the jinn."

He then proceeded to continuously recite the following verse:

تِلْكَ الدَّارُ الْاٰخِرَةُ نَجْعَلُهَا لِلَّذِيْنَ لَا يُرِيْدُوْنَ عُلُوًّا فِى الْاَرْضِ وَ لَا فَسَادًا وَ الْعَاقِبَةُ لِلْمُتَّقِيْنَ

"That [eternal] Home in the Hereafter We reserve for those who seek neither tyranny nor corruption on the earth. The ultimate outcome belongs to the righteous." [148]

---

147 *al-Zumar*, 39:10.

148 *al-Qaṣaṣ*, 28:83.

His wife sometime later entered his room once more, but this time she found him dead with his hand place on his face. ʿUmar ﷺ was found beaming with a brilliant smile, as if he was looking at his station in Paradise.

In a beautiful and succinct passage discussing the divine philosophy that informs the nature of this world and its status as an intermediate realm, the great gnostic Ibn ʿAṭāʾallāh al-Iskandarī ﷺ said:

جَعَلَكَ فِي العَالَمِ المُتَوَسِّطِ بَيْنَ مُلْكِهِ وَمَلَكُوتِهِ لِيُعْلِمَكَ جَلاَلَةَ قَدْرِكَ بَيْنَ مَخْلُوقَاتِهِ، وَأَنَّكَ جَوْهَرَةٌ تَنْطَوِي عَلَيْهَا أَصْدَافُ مُكَوَّنَاتِهِ

"He placed you in the middle realm between His physical world and His metaphysical world to inform you of the loftiness of your rank among his creatures. You are a gem merely enclosed by the shells of created forms."

The newborn who enters this world does so while crying whereas everyone around him is laughing and smiling in pleasure. But at the point of death, it is the opposite case for the believer: they leave the world laughing while everyone else around them cries. When a baby is born, they are given an *adhān* (call to prayer) without any *ṣalāh* (prayer), whereas when they pass away a *ṣalāh* is read over them without any *adhān*, which ultimately signifies the short duration of life in this temporal world.

Through His infinite Mercy, Allah ﷻ made almost every single cause of death a positive hallmark for the believer, and a means for facilitating their transition to Paradise with ease. Outwardly, some of these deaths may be unpleasant and painful, but they are replete with numerous rewards. As enumerated in the Hadith literature, there are a number of means through which a person can die and receive the reward of a *shahīd* (martyr) in the sight of Allah: 1) dying in a fire; 2) dying by drowning; 3) dying in a plague; 4) dying due to a stomach disease; 5) dying from a lung disease; 6) dying due to a road accident; 7) dying on a Friday; 8) dying while defending one's wealth; 9) dying while defending one's religion; 10) dying during pregnancy; and 11) dying during childbirth. Dying through one of these means signifies a righteous end for the believer and that they are loved by Allah ﷻ. In the sight of outsiders, these deaths may appear to be excruciating and indicative of an evil end. But in reality, the true beauty lies in where the soul of this person is heading to, which is a beautiful destination.

29

When life comes full circle

It is time to bid farewell to the departing soul. Its short stay over in this world is complete, and its appointed moment for reuniting with its Lord and the realm of the unseen has come. As the Angels carry the soul of the righteous person up into the heavens, the deceased's family prepare its dead body for the prescribed funeral rites. One beautiful verse of the Qur'an illustrates how Allah عَزَّ وَجَلَّ and His Angels eagerly await the ascent of the pious believer's soul after they pass away:

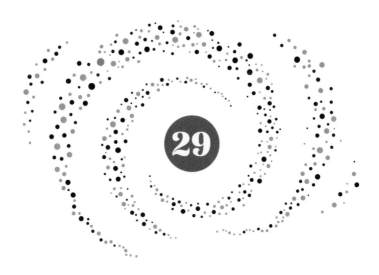

يَا أَيَّتُهَا النَّفْسُ الْمُطْمَئِنَّةُ ارْجِعِي إِلَى رَبِّكِ رَاضِيَةً مَرْضِيَّةً

"[Allah will say to the righteous:] 'O tranquil soul! Return to your Lord, well pleased [with Him] and well pleasing [to Him].'" [149]

As Muslims, we are all pleased with the regulations passed by Allah ﷻ and His supreme Decree. A common invocation which we are recommended to frequently recite is the following:

رَضِيتُ بِاللهِ رَبّاً وبِالإِسْلَامِ دِيناً وَبِمُحَمَّدٍ صَلَّى اللَّهُ عَلَيْهِ وَسَلَّمَ نَبِيّاً

"We are pleased with Allah as our Lord, with Islam as our religion, and Muhammad ﷺ as our Prophet."

But what does it mean to be pleased with Allah ﷻ as one's Lord? Imam Ibn al-Qayyim رحمه الله says that throughout the course of one's life, a Muslim undergoes three stages of *tawakkul* (reliance) in relation to their trust with Allah ﷻ. At first, one trusts Allah just as a person relies on their agent, whereby one attempts to maintain control and question them for every decision that they make. But with the passage of time, one begins to trust Allah ﷻ in a more deferential sense, such that they rely on Him just as a child views their mother. Then finally, one trusts Allah just as a dead body is fully subservient to its washer: it lets the latter turn its body whenever and however it wishes, without voicing any objections to the purification methods used. The final state of subservience is that which every believer internalizes

149 *al-Fajr,* 89:27-28.

during their stay on this Earth at one point of their life. When a believer dies, a new state of subservience and pure dependence becomes activated, which has a number of parallels with the stages they went through in this world. For one thing, when a person was born, they were completely helpless and required someone to wash, clothe, and feed them. During death, this absolute form of helplessness is reenacted, since one's loved ones will have to wash, shroud, and lower them into their final resting place.

As a person's soul starts to transition into the unseen realm known as the *barzakh*, it still has the capacity to view what is happening on the Earth. In an authentic Hadith, the Prophet ﷺ said that the deceased experiences pain if their relatives wail over them[150]; this is one of the reasons for why the practice of wailing and other ceremonial mourning sessions are prohibited in Islam. The dead thus can see and experience the actions of their family members at the earthly sphere, such as hearing the footsteps of their loved ones when they leave from their grave.[151] In one slightly-weak narration, it is reported that the Prophet ﷺ said:

إِنَّ الْمَيِّتَ يَعْرِفُ مَنْ يَحْمِلُهُ وَمَنْ يَغْسِلُهُ وَمَنْ يُدَلِّيهِ فِي قَبْرِهِ

"Verily, the dead one recognizes those who carry him, those who wash him, and those who lower him into his grave."[152]

150 *Sunan al-Tirmidhī*, 1002.

151 *Ṣaḥīḥ al-Bukhārī*, 1338.

152 *Musnad Imām Aḥmad*, 10614.

The astute and intelligent person prioritizes the Hereafter over this transient world, and ensures that they do not indulge in the temporary pleasures of this plane only to then experience an eternity of regret.

Some scholars have also reported that during the burial process, there is a special Angel that supervises the funeral rites and watches over it just as there is an Angel that accompanies a person before they are born. In this regard, ʿAmr ibn Dīnār ﵀ said:

مَا مِنْ مَيِّتٍ يَمُوْتُ إِلَّا وَرُوْحُه فِيْ يَدِ مَلَكٍ يَنْظُرُ إِلى جَسَدِه كَيْفَ
يُغَسَّلُ وَكَيْفَ يُكَفَّنُ وَ كَيْفَ يُمْشى بِه وَ يَجْلِسُ فِيْ قَبْرِه

"Not a single person dies except that his soul is in the hand of an Angel who observes his body, how it is washed, how it is shrouded, and how it is carried. It then enters into the grave to make sure that it is buried properly."[153]

The great Imam Abū al-Ḥasan al-Qābiṣī ﵀ reconciles the narrations which state that the soul will ascend to Paradise with those that affirm that it can see the events on Earth. In essence, he states that when the righteous souls ascend to the heavens and reach Allah ﷻ, He will say to them: "Go and see your place in Paradise." They will thus be provided the priceless opportunity to journey throughout the areas and levels of Paradise for the duration needed for washing their body.[154] This is one of the wisdoms being washing the dead body, since it purifies it and allows it to reach the level of cleanliness needed for entering and scouring the gardens of Paradise. This is analogous to how the heart of the blessed Prophet ﷺ was washed by Jibrīl ﵇ so that he could

153 al-Qurṭubī, *al-Tadhkirah*, p. 238.

154 al-Qurṭubī, *al-Tadhkirah*, p. 238.

be purified and prepared for conducting the special celestial journey known as *al-Isrā' wa al-Mi'rāj*. Thus, the more thorough and exacting the washing process is, the longer the time the soul has to explore the wonders and splendour of the permanent abode of bliss. But once the washing and shrouding process is complete, the soul returns once more to the temporal world. At this point, it wishes for its burial rites to be carried as soon as possible so that it may be freed from any constraints and explore the beautiful mysteries found in the *barzakh* stage. In a powerful narration, the Prophet ﷺ said:

إِذَا وُضِعَتِ الجَنَازَةُ وَاحْتَمَلَهَا الرِّجَالُ عَلَى أَعْنَاقِهِمْ فَإِنْ كَانَتْ صَالِحَةً
قَالَتْ: قَدِّمُونِي وَإِنْ كَانَتْ غَيْرَ صَالِحَةٍ قَالَتْ: يَا وَيْلَهَا أَيْنَ يَذْهَبُونَ بِهَا
يَسْمَعُ صَوْتَهَا كُلُّ شَيْءٍ إِلَّا الإِنْسَانَ وَلَوْ سَمِعَهَا الإِنْسَانُ لَصُعِقَ

"When the deceased is picked up and the men lift it onto their shoulders, if it was a righteous soul, it says, 'Hurry up and take me quickly, hurry up and take me quickly.' And if it was not a righteous person, it says, 'Woe to me, woe to me, where are you taking me?' Everything of the creation of Allah hears that cry except for the human beings around it. If they could hear that cry, they would faint."

This explains why the Prophet ﷺ urged his Muslim followers to perform the funeral rites with haste by stating:

أَسْرِعُوْا بِالْجَنَازَةِ

"Hurry up with the burial."

The Prophet ﷺ provided the rationale for this imperative by stating: "For if it is a righteous soul, you would bring it quicker to a beautiful abode and if it is otherwise it is an evil which you discard into the Earth."[155]

As the deceased person is being carried and taken to the grave, they will hear individuals speaking about their accomplishments and overall legacy, with some of these stories and tales being mentioned in order to comfort one another. Should they embellish an account or mention an inaccurate piece of information, the Angels will begin to interrogate the deceased person. The Prophet ﷺ said that in the case of the latter event, the Angels will poke the spirit of the dead person and say to him:

أَهَكَذَا كُنْتَ؟

"Were you as they claim you are?"

And just before the formal burial process commences, a major act of worship occurs, which is called *ṣalāh al-janāzah*,

155 *Ṣaḥīḥ Muslim*, 944.

or the funeral prayer. The attendees may include one's friends, family members, individuals that one had a mixed relationship, and even strangers. But they all band together in the prayer hall and attend the *ṣalāh al-janāzah* out of respect for the deceased, whereby they ask Allah ﷻ to shower them with His Mercy. Finally, after the prayer is finished, the Muslims move the deceased to the graveyard and bury the deceased in its allotted plot of land. Thus, humans return once more to their original source: the dirt from the ground, for as Allah ﷻ states:

مِنْهَا خَلَقْنَٰكُمْ وَفِيهَا نُعِيدُكُمْ وَمِنْهَا نُخْرِجُكُمْ تَارَةً أُخْرَىٰ

"From the earth We created you, and into it We will return you, and from it We will bring you back again."[156]

The burial process is complete, with the deceased's right side facing the Qiblah, which was the same direction they prayed towards throughout their life. Facing this sacred direction allows the heart to be oriented towards the One Who sent them to this world, such that they will be able to name Him when the Angels ask him them the following question:

مَنْ رَبُّكَ

"Who is your Lord?"

156 *Ṭā Hā*, 20:55.

Answering this question is no easy endeavour, which is why after the burial process the Prophet ﷺ would stand by the grave of the deceased and say:

إِسْتَغْفِرُوا لأَخِيكُمْ وَسَلُوا لَهُ التَّثْبِيتَ فَإِنَّهُ الآنَ يُسْأَلُ

"Ask Allah to forgive your brother and to make him steadfast, for he is now being asked."[157]

But just a few moments later, everyone will leave the deceased alone. But there is one major exception: one's family members. They will continue to pray to Allah ﷻ and ask Him to shower they deceased loved one with mercy. For this reason, when he was close to his death, 'Amr ibn al-'Āṣ ؓ ordered his children to remain by his grave after they buried him for the duration that it takes one to sacrifice an animal and distribute its meat. He provided the rationale for this order:

حَتَّى أَسْتَأْنِسَ بِكُمْ، وَأَنْظُرَ مَاذَا أُرَاجِعُ بِهِ رُسُلَ رَبِّي

"[Do this] so that I may feel your nearness and I can know what to answer my Lord's messengers with."[158]

Thus, one should not leave their loved one alone in their grave so quickly, as they will be remaining there until the Last Day. In addition, before they are questioned by the Angels, they will face another hurdle that is worthy of being mentioned. Just like how a person enters this world through a squeeze

---

157 *Sunan Abī Dāwūd*, 3221.

158 *Ṣaḥīḥ Muslim*, 121.

from their mother's womb, they will likewise be subjected to a squeeze when they enter the grave. In a Hadith, the Prophet ﷺ said that every deceased person who enters their final resting place will be subjected to a painful squeeze, where it will feel as if they are passing through a narrow passage. After going through this ordeal, they will face the ultimate test of answering the three questions that will be posed by the two interrogating Angels, which will ultimately revolve around three points: 1) Who was your Lord?; 2) Who was the one sent to you?; and 3) What was your way of life?

When the crying of your family members and friends ceases and their footsteps fade away, you will be left all alone in your grave, with nothing being there to distract you. At that point, you will have all the time needed to reflect on the legacy that you left behind and whether your life was a worthwhile experience. The astute and intelligent person prioritizes the Hereafter over this transient world, and ensures that they do not indulge in the temporary pleasures of this plane only to then experience an eternity of regret. They perform enough good deeds to earn a peaceful place in the Hereafter, such that they can enjoy an eternity of bliss. Only a fool would do the opposite, as stated by Ibn 'Aṭā'allāh al-Iskandarī ؒ:

إِحَالَتُكَ الأَعْمَالَ عَلَى وُجُودِ الفَرَاغِ مِنْ رُعُونَاتِ النَّفْسِ

"Your postponement of deeds till the time when you are free is merely one of the delusions of the self."

30

Did my life really matter?

The life that every person experiences in this world is stunningly short. Before one knows it, Allah ﷻ will call His servants back to their permanent abode. With this call, their temporal life will come to an end, just like how every episode of prayer concludes at a relatively fast pace. Every Muslim should hope and pray that when their soul is taken, Allah ﷻ greets them with contentment and with a message of peace.

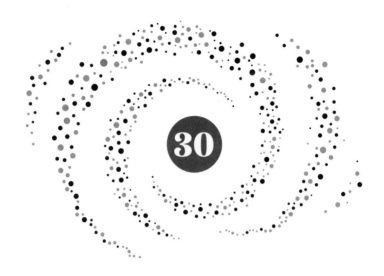

It is narrated that whenever ʿUmar ibn al-Khaṭṭāb ﷺ saw the Kaʿbah, he would say:

أَللّهُمَّ أَنْتَ السَّلَامُ وَ مِنْكَ السَّلَامُ فَحَيِّنَا رَبَّنَا بِالسَّلَامِ

"O Allah, You are peace and from You comes peace. So greet us, O our Lord, with peace."

As the funeral rites come to a close, one's family members, religious leaders, and community members give one final greeting of peace and pray that the same benevolent message is expressed by their Creator to their late loved one. At this point, the soul of the deceased has moved forward and will enter a new home, where it will be able to meet with their relatives and loved ones who passed before them. These relatives will be extremely pleased to meet this newly deceased member, since they will be eager to ask about all those left behind alive in the temporal world. Regarding this, the Prophet ﷺ said:

فَلَهُمْ أَشَدُّ فَرَحًا مِنَ أَهْلِ الغَائِبِ بِغَائِبِهِمْ

"The believing souls are more eager to receive you there than your long lost relatives [here on this Earth]."[159]

This sets the stage for a momentous intergenerational meeting. Grandparents who died before being able to see their grandchildren will now have the chance to meet them, and a distant ancestor from several generations prior might wish

---

[159] Al-Ḥākim, *al-Mustadrak*, 1302.

to see a virtuous person from their family line who appeared centuries later. The newly deceased person will be able to cheerily speak with its elders and share information about what happened in their life, the news of their children, and even relate to them the state of their living relatives. The recently deceased individual may also share moving stories about how a family friend that was struggling to end their immoral ways finally found the path to Allah ﷻ due to a pious deed they performed or a spiritual crisis that sparked their repentance. Meanwhile, these deceased individuals continue to benefit from their living relatives, who provide them spiritual gifts through their frequent words of *duʿā'* (supplication) to Allah ﷻ and the charity that they give in their name.

In this beautiful spiritual plane, righteousness transcends numerous generations and the spiritually upright people of the past connect with those who recently passed away. One may also enjoy the opportunity to connect with many of the past leaders and spiritual forefathers of their faith, such as the Companions ؓ and the blessed Prophet ﷺ himself. And this cycle may even repeat itself, such that, with the passage of time, one may be able to meet and correspond with members of the newer generation who pass away and enter the spiritual world as well. It may be an orphan that one sponsored and nurtured with material and religious assistance in the temporal world who passed away and now wishes to thank their supporter in the religious plane. Or it may be a nephew or niece that was about to trek a morally dubious path, but one intervened and provided them spiritual guidance.

But all of the aforementioned facts and information beg the ultimate question: was the life in this world really worth it, and did it really yield any meaningful benefits for oneself and others. The answer to this question will be evident for a person once they accrue the rewards for the good deeds that they performed in this life; it will cause them to be pleased with the decree that allowed them to live in this world in the first place, since it was the catalyst that facilitated the performance of good deeds. There are a myriad of good deeds whose rewards will reach a believer after they pass away. In a beautiful Hadith, the Prophet ﷺ said:

إِنَّ مِمَّا يَلْحَقُ الْمُؤْمِنَ مِنْ عَمَلِهِ وَحَسَنَاتِهِ بَعْدَ مَوْتِهِ عِلْمًا عَلَّمَهُ وَنَشَرَهُ وَوَلَدًا صَالِحًا
تَرَكَهُ وَمُصْحَفًا وَرَّثَهُ أَوْ مَسْجِدًا بَنَاهُ أَوْ بَيْتًا لِابْنِ السَّبِيلِ بَنَاهُ أَوْ نَهْرًا أَجْرَاهُ أَوْ
صَدَقَةً أَخْرَجَهَا مِنْ مَالِهِ فِي صِحَّتِهِ وَحَيَاتِهِ يَلْحَقُهُ مِنْ بَعْدِ مَوْتِهِ

"From among the rewards of the good deeds that will reach a believer after his death are knowledge which he taught and spread; a righteous child whom he left behind; a copy of the Qur'an that he bequeathed to someone else; a masjid that he built; a shelter that he built for the homeless or the wayfarers; a canal that he dug; or a type of charity that he gave during his lifetime when he was in good health, which now reaches him after his death."[160]

160 *Sunan Ibn Mājah*, 242.

A person will never be able to know their impact on the world until they see all of the entities and beings that testify on their behalf on the Day of Judgement. From one's own vantage point, the degree of positive influence that a person had may seem marginal, but in the sight of Allah ﷻ it is momentous. For example, one may consider the case of a Prophet who was unable to garner any followers when calling their people to Allah ﷻ. One may—as a preliminary judgement—deem this Prophet to play no constructive role in serving the true message of monotheism. But such a viewpoint is undoubtedly incorrect, since this Prophet did in fact play a constructive role; they likely served as a proof against their people or laid the groundwork for another Prophet to be sent after them. The blessed Prophet ﷺ described himself as being the last brick of a beautiful home, with every other brick of the structure representing a prior Prophet. Every prior Prophet played a decisive role in his positioning and placement as a Messenger of Allah in the Meccan plane. Thus, one should never underestimate the value of their deeds. In actual fact, they are seeds which will sprout and grow into countless blessings with the permission of Allah ﷻ.

There will come a point where a person will realize that every single moment of their life was worthwhile. Every person's life story—their accomplishments and failures, happy moments and sad ones—were written and decreed by the Lord 50,000 years before this world was even created, and then actualized in an orderly sequence at its destined moment. As Allah's servant, you mattered to the extent that He fashioned you and decreed for you a spot in this world in order to be a part of His story. The transient life in this universe is full of incredible moments, epiphanies, and rushes of faith from the heart that bear witness to His Greatness, Aid, Mercy, Forgiveness, Justice, Wisdom, and Love. Thus, in short, your portrait of a life was worth living, since throughout this entire process it was Allah ﷻ Who was creating and fashioning every moment.

The life of every person started with a scroll hanging from the Throne of the One Truth. After death, the soul of every righteous person seeks to attain close proximity to one of the chandeliers that are situated in that very Throne, so that it may return to its original home.

وَتَرَى ٱلْمَلَٰٓئِكَةَ حَآفِّينَ مِنْ حَوْلِ ٱلْعَرْشِ يُسَبِّحُونَ بِحَمْدِ رَبِّهِمْ
وَقُضِىَ بَيْنَهُم بِٱلْحَقِّ وَقِيلَ ٱلْحَمْدُ لِلَّهِ رَبِّ ٱلْعَٰلَمِينَ

"You will see the angels all around the Throne, glorifying the praises of their Lord, for judgment will have been passed on all with fairness. And it will be said, 'Praise be to Allah—Lord of all worlds!'"[161]

This verse encapsulates the story of humankind from its beginning all the way to its conclusion. When Adam عليه السلام was created and sneezed before the assembly of Angels, he said *alḥamdulillāh* (all praise is due to Allah). Likewise, when the blessed members of his progeny enter Paradise at the end, they will utter *alḥamdulillāh* as well. This beautiful culmination marks the success story of the believers, who will

161 *al-Zumar*, 39:75.

be handsomely rewarded by their Creator in the permanent abode of bliss. It was Allah's Decree for His pious slaves to be rewarded in the permanent gardens of the Hereafter, since this temporal world lacks the perfect attributes and stable features needed for attaining full enjoyment.

O Allah ﷻ, You are the Truth, and the One Who decrees in truth, purpose, wisdom, and justice. We ask You to infuse our decrees with mercy, wholesomeness, blessings, and the light of faith. O Allah ﷻ, we ask You to guide us to our other-worldly purpose in this temporal plane in a way that pleases You. O Allah, ﷻ we ask You to bless our families and provide us the means to remain connected with compassion and care, such that our homes are filled with joy and love.

O Allah ﷻ, we seek Your protection from dysfunctional family structures, from being the oppressor or the oppressed, as well as the trauma embedded in spiritually and morally bankrupt homes. O Allah ﷻ, provide us the inner strength, mental power, and endurance needed for us to overcome the limitations of our bodies, and allow us to be grateful for the health and soundness that You have bestowed upon us. O Allah ﷻ, make our souls beautiful and cause us to be concerned solely with the beauty of our character. O Allah ﷻ, just as You have made our appearances and bodies beautiful, make our souls and inner spiritual core even more beautiful. O Allah ﷻ, provide us the strength and patience to be content during times of poverty and gracious in times of prosperity.

O Allah ﷻ, allow our knowledge and faith to increase such that we possess firm conviction of Your presence. O Allah ﷻ, provide us pious and God-fearing spouses who fill our hearts and households with love, mercy, and tranquillity, and make our families the coolness of our eyes. O Allah ﷻ, provide us the power to rejuvenate ourselves after we are mentally broken, provide us comfort and healing whenever we become sick, and bless us with companionship whenever we become lonely. O Allah ﷻ, grant us all an honourable legacy that will be transmitted for many generations to come, and allow our standing in this world and the Hereafter to be morally upright. O Allah ﷻ, render our grey hairs a source of light and brightness in the Hereafter whereby they testify to our *īmān* (faith).

O Allah ﷻ, grant us all a sound ending and decree that our last words in this world to be *lā ilāha illa Allāh* (there is no god but Allah). O Allah ﷻ, ease the suffering of the Muslims throughout the globe: satisfy their needs, settle their debts, provide shelter to the homeless, eradicate the diseases of the sick ones, provide relief to the distressed, destroy their oppressors, provide guidance to those who are lost, and provide Your light to those who are submerged in the depths of darkness. O Allah ﷻ, fill our hearts with certainty such that we have the strength to confront any adversity with resilience, to overcome any hurdles, to illuminate any dark segment with the light of our faith, and to truly witness the wisdom behind Your Decree and appreciate why You created us in this world.

Final reflection

By Dr. Zohair Abdul-Rahman

So the answer to the question of "why me?" is **"you will only find out as you live your story seeking Allah at every moment."**

1. Let the days do as they please.
Let your soul be calm over what He decrees.

2. Do not become impatient over the calamities of the night.
For there is no pain in this world that maintains its might.

3. Be a person that abates his fears and his freight.
Make your nature one of generosity and doing what's right.

4. If all your flaws and faults were to be exposed,
You would wish concealment so no one knows.

5. So conceal your faults and flaws with excellence,
For every embarrassment is overshadowed by benevolence.

6. Don't show weakness in front of your enemy.
Indeed his gloating spells your calamity .

7. Don't expect generosity from the greedy.
For fire never gives water to those who are needy.

8. Wealth is not decreased by your idle inability,
Nor is it increased by your perceived capability
(increased activity).

9. There is no sorrow that remains nor happiness that
lasts eternally (is everlasting).
Your hardships will fade and so will your prosperity
(thriving).

10. When you develop a content and tranquil heart,
Then you and the wealthiest of this world cannot
be set apart.

11. Whoever is afflicted with a decreed calamity,
No land or sky can protect him from its eventuality.

12. Though the land of Allah is vast and plentiful,
The decree can never be preventable.

13. So do not rely on your days that often betray,
For there is no cure that can avail from death on that day.

O Allah ﷻ, grant us all a sound ending and decree that our last words in this world to be lā ilāha illa Allāh (there is no god but Allah). With the light of our faith, allow us to truly witness the wisdom behind Your Decree and appreciate why You created us in this world.